Teaching foreign languages in schools

the Silent Way

Caleb Gattegno

Educational Solutions
New York City

All materials described in this book
can be obtained from
Educational Solutions, Inc.
80 Fifth Avenue
New York, N.Y. 10011

© C. Gattegno 1963, 1972
First published 1963
Second Edition published 1972
Reprinted 1978
Printed in the United States of America
SBN: 87825 046 8

CONTENTS

ACKNOWLEDGEMENTS

This book has been prepared by Mira Nikolić Erickson from the original text published in England in 1963, and from a number of articles contributed by teachers who studied at my seminars and workshops and who have used the Silent Way in their own language teaching.

Ms. Erickson's contribution can be found on every page of the main part of the book. She had to clarify much of the original which, as a scientific document, did not attempt to meet the needs of all readers. It is an improved text that respects the value of the contribution of a long investigation in language teaching.

Each of the contributors of the articles in the Appendix has been thanked personally. Here I want to reiterate my gratitude for these additions that make the book more readable.

PREFACE TO THE NEW EDITION

When this book appeared in the United Kingdom, in 1963, it only received two very cursory reviews in the press, both of them in the United States, although copies were sent to all major magazines for language teachers.

Since then, three thousand volumes have been purchased and presumably read. The proposals that the book contains have found a place in texts which are required reading for teachers. An eager audience emerged among teachers of languages in private and public schools, colleges and universities.

There were no references to the existing literature in the original book, because it was basically a summary of the findings of one person whose many years of investigation were devoted to the study of language learning and teaching. The content of the text was a set of propositions which expressed what the author alone saw in the field he was contemplating.

A number of readers who have since shared with the author their responses to these propositions found them completely new. However, it is not the novelty that makes them valuable, but rather the fact that they offer solutions to some problems which have created serious obstacles in language learning.

The general view expressed so far seems to be that the proposals made in this book work much better than any other currently available, because for the first time the learners in their concreteness are taken into account.

This is a completely new idea in education. It was much easier to be concerned with languages and their steadiness than with moody and unpredictable boys and girls, and men and women whose appearances revealed nothing about their functionings. Hundreds of philologists and linguists have produced grammars and language courses over the past centuries, and the time to study these writings distracted from a study that could only be valid if conducted in the classroom, while teaching.

Now that there is a beginning of this proper study, and that some of its findings which can mark the path for further venture are available, teachers are coming to the realization that if there is a job to be done, and it needs to be done as well as possible, why not join the team that is at work on that path. Hence, today, without heralding or ushering, we have accumulated evidence which shows that there is a distinctly better way of teaching foreign languages, known to the initiated as the *Silent Way*.

The evidence resulted from the experimental teaching, first without the printed materials, without any materials, in fact, but a set of colored rods. The people ranged from those who had almost no idea what it was to teach in this way to those who had a pretty good idea, since they had been students of one or more languages through the Silent Way. The languages which have been tried out are more numerous than the ones for which we have prepared the materials, and these are still more numerous than those for which the materials are completed. They are, in alphabetic order: Arabic, Brazilian, Portuguese, Cantonese, Danish, English, Farsi, French, German, Hebrew, Hindi, Hungarian, Italian, Japanese, Mandarin, Russian, Serbo-Croatian, Spanish, Thai.

All age groups, from preschoolers to retired executives, have been involved in the experiments and all have taught us something vital. We have come to a realization that it is a vain enterprise to think of writing a teacher's guide for the Silent Way. Hence, in spite of the repeated promise that a teacher's guide would be published, it neither materialized so far nor will it be the case in the future.

Something valuable was gathered in taping a large number of classes in two or three languages. These tapes provide a vivid display of the activity of a class with a silent teacher who finds the guide he needs for the successive steps in what the students offer in their responses. Naturally, these audio-tapes do not supply the visual elements which are so important for an understanding of the lessons. Those who have sat in classes taught by this approach will easily imagine what went on in association with what they hear. But others may be totally lost. Video-tapes are gradually eliminating this undesirable possibility.

The revised text of the original is reproduced here. There was need for a more extensive revision, but this would have delayed the appearance of the book which is out of print.

Almost ten years have elapsed since the text was written and most of it is as valid today as it was originally. The very few of its unfulfilled promises fall into two categories: those which, even if unfulfilled, do not make the approach any less effective (teacher's guide), and those towards whose fulfillment some steps have been taken (development of materials). Because a sufficient number of people are now involved in the expansion and exploration of the Silent Way, there is no doubt that the coming years will see an increase in the materials offered, after it has been found that they meet the needs of the students.

The new appendix of this book includes short contributions by some of those who have used the Silent Way in classrooms. These contributions were requested in order to hear voices other than that of the inventor, and to allow the teachers who are looking at the Silent Way to get some testimony from the users themselves.

I hope that this preface, the revised text, and the appendices will make the new book into a more handy tool for the teachers of languages. But the actual living of the approach through learning a new language remains still the best introduction. In our schools we offer three day courses of 21 hours and one-week courses of 40 hours. Both weekend and weeklong seminars are given at two or three levels. The intensity of the learning and the shortness of the course seem to complement each other, and a vast majority of the students have expressed satisfaction that the formula takes care of many obstacles previously experienced in language learning.

But even in courses in schools and colleges where the intensity is restricted to some 40 minutes a day, for so many days a week, it has been found that a good teacher of the Silent Way manages to create a continuity that neither weekends nor short or long vacations seem to affect adversely. Languages show themselves as new experiences to be acquired rather than lists to be remembered.

It is our deep belief that the science of education which is in the making — since the recognition of our premise that the only thing that can be educated in man is his awareness — has already made a definite contribution to the teaching of languages, and that the scene has radically changed since the Silent Way has been adopted.

New York City
September 1972

FOREWORD

This book is written after many years of study, reflection and experimentation in varying conditions and places. The first part of its double title reflects the intention to restrict the discussion to what can be done in schools, not attempting to include all cases of language teaching, in particular individual solitary learning. The second part tells of a way which at first may seem paradoxical, but I hope will appear to the reader as he advances in the book increasingly as a sensible approach, and one that is more akin than other attitudes to the challenges of language learning.

It seemed to me that the time had arrived for me to put together my experiences of the last thirty-five years or so, in which I have been actively engaged in studying languages, coaching private pupils and testing my ideas with classes in Argentina, Brazil, Canada, Egypt, England, Ethiopia, Fiji, India, Israel, Spain, Thailand, Uruguay, U.S.A. and Yugoslavia. My experiments were designed to test sometimes techniques of acceleration of learning, sometimes hypotheses about how difficulties are met by people of different linguistic backgrounds, sometimes an intuition about what could help learners over apparently insuperable hurdles, but always to test my progress in the grasp of what language learning is. I hope to have been able, every time I encountered a new light, to sensitize myself to it, and I hope I have not wasted most opportunities that came my way in the varied conditions in which I worked. The reader will decide whether I have done justice to the factors that impinge upon learners engaged in acquiring languages, as well as whether I have been able to gain new insights into the true challenges and to keep a check on the play of prejudices.

The unfolding of the argument in this book is as follows.

Having come to the conclusion that the learning of a foreign language is in many respects radically different from the learning of the mother tongue, I analyse the latter in the first chapter and try to show that a foreign language can in schools only be learnt by artificial methods, employing materials constructed for the purpose.

The experiments mentioned above have led to the use of existing materials and the creation of others that permit a constant control upon their uses. But they have also led to techniques which made it possible for the teacher to say less and less as the lessons advanced, while the pupils were saying more and more and using their own inner criteria developed in this approach. Because of this feature, it was decided to call it the *Silent Way*, so that from the start the public would be informed that it presents a radically different approach to language teaching.

So far, the people who have witnessed the experiments have agreed that the inspiration of this approach owes little to the "methods" already in use. They also agree that it stimulates the linguistic powers of people who believed that they would never be able to acquire a new language, that it mobilizes their consciousness to such a degree that, often in a matter of minutes, they are certain that the way is open for them and that it is only a matter of time and no longer of ability. Observers also agree that because the circumstances selected for the experiments were supposed to be the least favourable, even better results than the (often spectacular) ones witnessed can be expected when more normal conditions prevail. The experimentor was a stranger to the children; there were a number of observers in the class (sometimes as many as one hundred); the experimentor was teaching up to eighty pupils, or the lowest stream of an age group, or after school hours, or a language that he does not know as a native, or a single sample lesson all too short or crowded and using improvised means.

Because of these facts and the opinions of critical colleagues whose academic knowledge far exceeds that of the author, it was thought opportune to make available *now* the materials of this *Silent Way. Now* that audio-visual techniques are crowding the market and attracting so much attention, a healthy antidote may be found in an approach that throws the learner upon himself, that eliminates as far as possible the mechanical elements of teaching and learning, and minimizes the conditioning of the learners. Since an author and a publisher are only successful when what they propose is accepted, tested and cherished by the users (here the teachers of languages), the moment is opportune for this publication just because of the uphill struggle that faces a proposal like the one made in this book and embodied in the materials offered with it. If, in the present circumstances, we can convince teachers that we have something to offer, this will prove at the same time that what we offer is worthwhile. It will also permit us to say that we have made a contribution to education, since we have set teachers on new paths where so much remains to be discovered.

The readers will soon find that I have not attempted to reduce the magnitude of the challenges, that I am really concerned with remaining in reality, and that I am ready to take hints from wherever they come. This may produce a picture of the situation which is neither clear nor simple. If it is true that we know little about what confronts us, would it help to believe that we know much? If in order to solve a difficult problem we replaced it by a simpler but irrelevant one, would we be better off? I claim that the discussions in this text will contain as much of the reality as I can meet in my mind, keeping at the centre of my preoccupation all relevant facts, however difficult it is to think of them in the complex situation. If this produces a text that is difficult to follow by an immediate scanning of the lines, the only remedy is to read it slowly and to discuss it at length. At least readers will know that they are taken into the author's confidence and told everything that appears to him of significance and importance, rather than given a watered-down version of what little he knows.

While I believe that this new approach has much to commend it, and while I very much hope that it will be given as fair a trial as my previous suggestions to colleagues in schools, I must point out that it is a one man proposal based on one man's experience, of necessity limited, and that the most important contribution of this work is the opening of new vistas in education that should excite a new generation of people to investigate and to experiment with what they find behind the doors that are now put ajar.

READING, ENGLAND

April, 1963

1.

The Subordination of Teaching to Learning in the Case of Foreign Languages

In this book an attempt will be made to adapt to the teaching of foreign languages a new spirit which has already been sucessfully tried out in the teaching of mathematics, and reading and writing in the mother tongue.

This new spirit is now expressed in a general phrase: the subordination of teaching to learning. Its full meaning will emerge slowly and its significance will be completely understood if and when the reader accepts experimental lessons as the correct test of its validity.*

*See the Appendix: The Silent Way in the Classroom.

From the study of the literature concerned with educational research, it is clear that very rarely have there been attempts at knowing what learning actually entails, particularly the learning of human beings engaged in complex activities. Yet the millions of people who are daily engaged in learning, and other millions in teaching, could have gathered the relevant material and evidence to guide the teaching profession towards a deeper awareness of what there is to be done to improve teaching and learning.

I have devoted most of my professional efforts to the study of learning in the various fields in which I have been involved. As an experimentor in education, I have tried out, in varying circumstances, hypotheses and materials suggested by previous analyses of situations. Working for years in different environments, I have been able to discover much that I believe can be of assistance to colleagues everywhere. This book is a further contribution to the task of understanding what we can do to improve our grasp of the challenges met in education. The topic chosen here is the study of foreign languages.

Though I have tried to study a score of them, my experience is naturally very limited, and some of the conclusions may not hold if the languages I have considered are replaced with others which I do not know. Throughout this text, I shall endeavor to be watchful in order to minimize shifts from the particular to the general in cases where this would mean violation of reality.

One thing seems obvious, and that is, that the hardest language to learn, of all foreign languages, is the mother tongue. This is because a baby, lacking so much of what he will possess at the end of the process, has to make sense of noises that are conventions used to replace meanings. Meanings are rarely fully conscious in the minds of the users of languages. Still, most of us have managed to learn our mother tongue well enough at the tender age of two-plus to appear to use it accurately in communicating with others in our environment.

Another point that is clear to me is that the apprenticeship in the mother tongue cannot be described accurately by the words *imitation* or *practice* — which simply hide our ignorance of what actually takes place. Having been privileged to study carefully this apprenticeship of at least one child, I can only say that such study is probably the best school for language learning investigators. Everything is magnified here and made much easier to observe *so long as one does not start with a projection of one's own preconceived ideas.* To bring fixed ideas to the study of how learning takes place is a sure way of missing most points presented to us by the learners. Observers who have truly described aspects of the process of learning the mother tongue found a confirmation of their conclusions, even though they employed various research techniques and means of study.

In this introduction it may be permissible to report briefly on what I have found important for all students of language learning.

A close examination of the ways in which we acquire our first language will throw light at some phenomena seldom observed by investigators.

A baby is such a mysterious being in the way he uses his time up to the age when his actions and words are accessible to adults, that most of what we know about him is doubtful. Still, it is obvious that he uses his time to grow in awareness of himself and of the environment, and that no awareness of the world is possible before the means to become aware of it exist in a child. This statement tells the reader that I do not share the view that the environment has its ways of organizing minds by impinging upon them, by making deeper and deeper impacts and leaving to a mysterious law the job of co-ordinating impressions into a meaningful whole which works automatically once formed. I can only accept as true that, from birth, a child's mind equips itself more and more adequately by its own working, trial and error, and deliberate experimentation; by suspending judgment and revising conclusions. This is done (in turn and also simultaneously) by the tools of perception, the tools of making sense and of discovering truth, the tools of expression, the tools of transformation, the tools of making sense of deferred experience, of symbols, of various areas of living, of ever-increasing complex experiences involving all that is reached and reachable, or inaccessible though immanent.

Anyone sensitive enough recognizes this to be his own case. His inability to give a date of the appearance of these dimensions in his own mind, suggests an implicit agreement that it may have been a quality from birth. Anyone who has really watched small children, and not merely forced them into the preconceived mold of a theory, also knows that the working of their minds is affected by the co-presence, in them and in the environment, of experiences in the realms of affectivity, of the senses (outer and inner), of the body image, of the intellect, and of so many other inaccessible components. Anyone who studies knowing reaches the conclusion that not all our experiences are as clear, as precise, as devoid of uncertainty as we would wish them to be, and the intuitions in all directions constantly guide us in meeting the unknown that surrounds us.

If this is true of man's way of knowing, it cannot fail to be present when babies try to meet the unknown represented by the mother tongue. A baby does it on his own, and successfully.

Language users in the baby's environment are, on the whole, unaware of his means and of what he is doing with himself at any one stage. Adults cannot begin to understand the process of his learning until there is an opening which is accessible to them, such as imitation. This is accepted as explanation of how babies learn, because it is a tool for the adult, and because babies sometimes seem to use it. But to state that babies learn by imitation is, to say the least, an abuse of the circumstances. A more correct statement would be: we begin to enter the mystery of the learning done by a baby when we find him using tools for knowing that appear similar to what we do when we say that we imitate. Before that we cannot reach him. Nevertheless, because of scientific theory and the idea of evolution, one would say that there must be an order of precedence in the elaboration of these tools by the mind, and that by studying this process we may push back the frontiers that separate the mystery from our grasp of it.

Since all observers state that children learn by imitation, and since it is clear that what children ultimately know is the language of the environment and not another language, it is claimed that the grasp of the language must be through an effort by the learner to produce what the environment uses. This is what is covered by the word "imitation." Common sense tells us that what was not there at a certain stage is now available, so it must have arisen somehow; the production of sounds recognizably the same as those made by other people must be achieved by doing what others do in order to produce them. Is that not imitation?

While agreeing that the final stages of the apprenticeship in the mother tongue could be described in that way, I do not think that we are really making any progress in our understanding of language learning by stopping at such an explanation. For it is equally accessible to the observer to see that babies, long before they utter words, spend long sessions in studying their own sound production, becoming aware of what to do for what purpose, what varying pitch and intensity are, what is involved in running breath over the tongue, through the lips, against the inner membranes of the mouth, through the larynx and the nose. They study their own crying and modulate it to achieve their purpose. They produce *sounds* before they can change the *noises* they hear into recognizable sounds. Sounds are meaningful as such to them before they can process any environmental noises and attempt to attach a meaning to each. Indeed it is open to all observers to note that as soon as a baby can produce a sound, someone in the environment produces it by *imitating the baby.* This is to my mind an important observation for the student of the learning of the mother tongue. Babies are busy with their own problems of sound production, and someone who happens to be near them realizes that they are saying *da* or *dada*, or *ma* or *mama* and goes on repeating it, thus engendering the cycle indispensable for the learning of the mother tongue. Indeed, it is the repetition by other people of sounds made by the baby that gives him the objective component that a sound he can produce is of significance in the environment. This cycle will be repeated a number of times, making a child select from among the large number of sounds he can make those that are current among the speakers around him. Of all the possible sounds he is capable of making, he is restricting himself to producing more frequently those that seem to have an echo in the environment. It is the imitation by other people of some of the sounds produced by babies that channels the production of some sounds of the mother tongue. This is not learning of what exists, but agreeing to separate a set of noises among all possible noises because of the feedback that the language environment provides.

When enough of these echoed sounds are available and at the disposal of a baby, a new situation arises. A child can now recognize that some of the things he spontaneously produces have a different kind of existence. They are objectively produced by others as well as by himself. He can now use this bridge to cross from his experience to theirs and back. He is assisted by the environment in that

6

no absolute matching of the sounds he produces with those produced by the environment is required for acceptance. This is a second observation of import. Production of sounds being spontaneous, and similarity of these sounds with those of the environment being only approximate, babies do not feel the compulsion to alter their own activity to agree with an outer criterion. Parents and others not only tolerate what the baby makes available but also delight at the recognition of some quality in the sounds he produces that can open up communications with the little one. This creates excellent background for further experimentation and improvement of the tools he has. No one ever dreams of getting socially acceptable responses at once, and we contribute goodwill in changing a nondescript sound into a meaningful request, order or indication. Therefore, a baby finds in the environment a situation that will not overtax his powers, nor defeat the spontaneous activity of making and matching noises. Babies learn to talk, and do not often show signs of distress or anxiety.

Children pass from their solitary experimentation with sound production, sound hearing, and the matching of sounds heard and sounds uttered, to the social exercise of recognizing sounds independently of pitch, intensity, timbre or emotional context. This indicates that the first stage of learning the mother tongue is both an activity of a gigantic magnitude and one that does not unduly tax the powers of babies.

Learning to talk the mother tongue presents many phases after this shift. The baby is now aware of the symbolic role of language and has to acquire the mechanism by which he can become more and more definite in his communication, if he wants to obtain from the environment responses that correspond to his intentions.

While learning to utter one-word sentences, he is submitted to whole-sentence patterns, to statements that carry emotional contents. Little has been written about the melodic support of language learned by babies. Yet it is a common observation that mothers and other people in contact with babies do not take precautions when addressing them. They use the language that is available to them to state all they wish to say as completely as when talking among themselves. Babies and older children are actually submitted to a flow of words knitted together by the sustaining meaning and coming from the mouth as an integrated whole. Before the words are grasped for what they are, the melody unifying the statement reaches the ear and structures time. It seems that living language, when spoken, strikes the listener first through an integrative schema of its non-verbal components: the ups and downs, the stressed and unstressed, compact or loose, intense or relaxed elements which constitute the melody of a language as opposed to its vocabulary. Vocabularies are concerned with analytic experience, melody with synthetic; and the synthetic, the intuitive, precedes the analytic. Babies and children know what a sentence tells them long before they can utter its contents. For utterance, they need new tools that take time to be forged. Thus, children understand more than they can express, because the containers of the words, i.e., the integrative schemata of meaning and structure reach them before the details can be singled out, and also because man's language is only partly made of words. Whatever language is, it is certainly a substitute for experience, so experience is what gives meaning to language. Language becomes functional only when it carries meaning to the hearer. And much of its meaning is carried first through intonation, intensity and other melodic elements besides words.

The normal analytical powers of babies, already challenged at birth and constantly called upon to sort things out, are soon brought into play. They are used first to distinguish, then to classify, then to notice how words behave when used by the surrounding speakers, and finally to check whether responses fit in with the requests made by using sounds whose meaning is uncertain. Babies actually do consciously all this and more. How could one learn to talk adequately otherwise?

It is remarkable that babies know that words cover classes of objects. Their use of words without anxiety is a clear indication that their normal attitude of suspended judgment, which is necessary when entering an alien world full of things created by others, helps them to associate a class of events with each sound. No word by itself can convey precise meaning. To reach meaning, we need to act upon classes by taking what mathematicians call their *intersection* and logicians their *conjunction.* If we take each word of a sentence alone, we find that it covers a class of possible respondents. The class is progressively restricted so that ultimately we reach a stage where ambiguity can be avoided. This is the way we use language, and to use it properly requires that we learn the game of restricting the possible respondents of a class. It is to that end that children spend the third stage of their apprenticeship in language learning. Starting with nouns that cover classes of objects, they manage to acquire a vocabulary referring to things that can be perceived and pointed at. It would be a mistake to imagine that the names of objects are not abstract categories. They are in fact as abstract as any other comprehensive category, for it is the class-content that represents the abstraction. It should be emphasized that, because of the existence of a perceptible dimension for the elements of a class, perception is used directly to help sort out without words, a situation that can also be verbalized. It is this additional quality of perceptibility of a situation and not the absence of abstraction which will make it, at a certain stage, distinct from others, which will be called "abstract" because of the absence of such an immediate respondent: for example, in the case of "goodness" or "beauty".

Babies' and children's vocabularies develop according to

their powers of moving from wider classes to more restricted ones, and not from the particular to the general, as is often stated. The particular is highly structured, and is therefore richer in attributes which require a larger vocabulary to be properly described, while the elements forming a class may have attributes that are ignored. Compare: "a glass" and "the green glass that is on the mantlepiece in our living room," and the difference between the particular and the general will at once come out. We can safely say then that children's actual way of learning speech is from the general to the more and more particular.

Much of what has been observed concerning babies gains a different light if seen from this angle. For example, while acquiring his language, a baby at first uses one-word sentences which are mainly nouns. "Papa" and "Daddy" apply to all objects that have more apparent similarities than apparent differences. This is because "papa" describes a class and is not yet restricted to an individual. But the same baby calls "papa" an impression he has of someone who changes clothes, color of garments, posture, size with distance, thus indicating that each individual is a class for him, because of all the attributes that are present, noticed sometimes and ignored in other circumstances.

Because of this capacity of babies to operate mentally at the level of class and algebra of classes, we cannot escape the conclusion that learning to talk is one of the surest indications that children are at ease in at least one highly intellectual activity. We have been dismally mistaken in our psychology of children when we assumed that young age means rudimentary experience of little significance.

To sum up this brief discussion of the apprenticeship in the mother tongue, we can say that it has taught us:

1. That man, as an essentially intellectual being, naturally considers classes of events and objects before

reaching particular objects or events. Otherwise he would not be able to learn to talk.

2. That learning to talk means structuring the successive intersections of a multiplicity of unstructured classes so as to produce a particular class.

3. That this activity can take place because of the awareness that experience, with all its complexities, is to be grasped before words and their correspondents.

4. That in spoken speech the melodic integrative schemata are a more primitive experience of language than the words, and are perceived much earlier than the words.

5. That anyone who has learned to talk his mother tongue to an environmentally satisfactory level is endowed with mental powers that are, to say the least, sizeable.

6. That to learn the mother tongue is an extraordinary achievement because it has been done without help from others and without the assistance of the tools which will be available at the end of the apprenticeship. There follows, up to a point, a necessary course imposed by the circumstances of meeting the true unknown with no prior training. This course is not a strain because of the attitude of suspended judgment on the part of children.

7. That once the problems of that apprenticeship are resolved, no child remains the same, and cannot learn another language in the same way because of what he now knows.

In the section above, much of what I gained through observing children learn their mother tongue has been reported.* However, it is my last point that I think we must take most seriously in studying the learning of a new language.

The learning of a new language is considered to be that of a foreign language (when it is not normally in circulation in the environment). People talk of the "natural" way of learning, and of the "direct way" of teaching, referring somehow to a way similar to that of a baby learning his mother tongue. It is my contention that we shall not score much success if we continue in that way since circumstances in the learner are on the whole incomparable with those prevailing in the first case.

If it is true that a new language will require from the learner a new adaptation, it is equally true that apprenticeships in the mother tongue and in a foreign language have little in common. In the former, a baby has no clue of what to do to reach meaning in words; in the latter, the learner has acquired a language and knows what languages are for. Consciously or unconsciously, he brings with him training in the association of sounds and situations, structures and meanings, intonation and quality of experience, sets of words and particular experience: perceptible attributes as well as words for concepts several stages removed, symbols, images, etc. He knows how to produce a verbal stream and to find in it the power of expression, the necessity of expression — mechanisms that ensure that what is said is adequate to the purpose, etc.

That all this is more unconscious than conscious is relevant in this discussion, since it can be proved that consciousness of one's own earlier activity can be brought to throw light upon the whole of the learning process.

My proposal is to replace a "natural" approach by one that is very "artificial" and, for some purposes, strictly

*In a book on the baby's ways of knowing (to appear in 1973) this study is taken much further.

controlled, and to use all that there is to be tapped in every mind in every school.

As a teacher, I know that no proposal of mine can be successful unless it really meets the requirements of classroom situations. It will be really successful (1) if I have taken into account the problems teachers of language meet in their own minds and in their training; (2) if I have made allowance for the capabilities of students, their habits and expectations, the demands of circumstances, etc.; (3) if I have not followed my own bent when suggesting a course, but have made my materials as flexible as will be required by the variety of conditions in the schools where languages are taught.

As I developed my techniques while subordinating my teaching to the learning, I found that I could very early transfer the responsibility for the use of the language to my students, so that I became able to teach using fewer and fewer words. It is this aspect of my techniques of teaching that prompted me to call the approach *The Silent Way of Teaching Foreign Languages.* If there is one feature I value in my approach, it is well described by the word "silent," since it will convey at once that there are means of letting the learners learn while the teacher stops interfering or side-tracking. Scores of teachers who are using the Silent Way recognize silence* to be one of the powerful tools in their teaching.

To conclude this chapter, I will give an overall view of the techniques and the materials developed to achieve what is described above.

I assume that we start with people who already possess verbal consciousness and an unconscious readiness to use words to describe a situation. They know how to associate

*For a more detailed discussion on this matter, see the Appendix.

13

definite words with different circumstances. I will consider myself free to use intuitive means and to expect communication even if, from a strictly logical viewpoint, doubts can be raised as to whether what I suggest would work. In contrast to a baby's learning, I will use as few nouns as I can — for a long while only one. Contrary to the common suggestion, I will endeavor to get a maximum yield of linguistic awareness out of a minimal vocabulary, stressing melody, natural expression, variations on one theme, and the dictation of sentences spoken only once with a natural intonation (this after the written word has been introduced).

Contrary to common practice, the oral work introduced in the beginning is quite early followed by writing, using charts with words shown in colors to convey their phonetic equivalent. This provides the learners with new facilities for practicing the melody of the language while using a visual code.

Again, contrary to common practice, the learners are not asked to learn a list of words by heart, for the extension of the language takes different courses at different stages. In all cases memory tracks are replaced by recognition and familiarity. Students are allowed to try their hands and to make mistakes in order to develop their proper criteria of rightness, correctness and adequacy.

Once again, contrary to common practice, correcting is only seldom part of the teacher's work. The existing knowledge of what language is about, and the planning of the lessons in such a way that they allow the development of inner criteria, will be sufficient for achieving correctness. There will be no need for the teacher's approval or use of deferred criteria such as dictionaries or grammars.

No use is made of phonetic spellings. Instead, the coloring of the words* on the charts indicates the

---

*Readers acquainted with *Words in Color*, the method of teaching reading and writing in the mother tongue, know that colors are used on letters or groups of letters to convey similarity or difference of sounds.

appropriate sounds in a color-code that serves as many languages as can be, thus providing bridges between the phonetics of the various languages. For each language a colored "phonic code" or *Fidel* is proposed, representing all the sounds of a language and all the different spellings if the language is not a phonetic one. The charts for the *Fidel* serve a number of purposes, of which the enhancement of word consciousness is not the least.

The complementary material of worksheets, with exercises that employ the imagination of the learners and provide opportunities to widen the lessons learned at school, serve to individualize learning and to allow students to work at their own pace.

Tapes and discs are already widely used in language learning. Here, however, we use recordings of speech in foreign languages to train the ear in the differences between language melodies and in the various expressions of emotion and mental attitudes. This is done by asking learners to listen to passages in many different languages presented at random. Later in the recording, the same passages are grouped according to their similarity or dissimilarity, so that finer distinctions between the melody of each can be perceived. Further recordings give examples of good speech in the language being studied.

The complete set of materials is at present intended to include:

- A set of colored wooden rods
- A set of wall charts containing words of a "functional" vocabulary and some additional ones; a pointer for use with the charts in Visual Dictation
- A phonic code chart(s) (Fidel)
- Tapes or discs, as required
- Drawings and pictures, and a set of accompanying worksheets
- Transparencies and a second set of worksheets

15

- Three texts: sentences to be read separately; sentences to be read consecutively; a Book of Stories
- Worksheets on the whole language, without any restrictions
- Three anthologies
- Films

Two last remarks. It is my experience that the basic materials are acceptable to students from 7 years of age on. Only the "Readers" may need adaptation to age. It is also my experience that in one school year, at the rate of one period a day, a sufficient amount of the foreign language will be mastered to permit either deeper studies in that language in the following years, or the attack of another language each year, leading to a level of knowledge that any school teacher would consider honorable in the present state of teaching. Perhaps in our modern world, where people mix so freely, this level of knowledge of several languages is by far preferable to a better knowledge of one only.

2. The Spirit of a Language

In this chapter, we will leave the problems of teaching in the background, and concentrate on some observations made on languages. This, I believe, is necessary in any realistic discussion of the components of language learning.

Although every generation of adults adds only a little to their mother tongue, leaving a heritage which is scarcely changed from generation to generation, except perhaps with respect to new words, it is clear that languages have changed over the centuries. To trace alterations is a specialist's job. To recognize major influences is less difficult. Most linguists have some idea of what has happened to the languages they know during the last four or five centuries. Maybe no one should attempt to teach a language who has not reflected on these matters and has not gained some understanding of the idiosyncrasies of the language he has to teach.

It is perhaps as pertinent to require that teachers of

languages consider other components of the linguistic situation.

For anyone who has learned a number of languages and has studied different cultures of their users one important matter seems to emerge. In their environments and through the events that form their history, human beings have attempted to objectify a conscious or unconscious collective aim and have submitted their minds, their passions, and their visions to the effects of a larger molding force. Peoples have learned to adhere, through their education, to most of the implicit or explicit aims of their society. One of the tools for such education is the assimilation of the mother tongue. Languages are excellent witnesses of various modes of thought. The spirit of each language seems to act as a container for the melody and the structure of the language and most users are unconscious of it. Words may be dropped or have their meaning changed, but it does not seem thinkable that the English or the Germans will ever agree to change the way in which they form the future of their verbs and adopt the one used by the Latin countries — or conversely.

Expressions that are more telling in one language than in another may be adopted by writers in their work, but the number of these expressions must remain small lest communication with those who do not know them is endangered.

Because we find simultaneously a vein that is maintained in the history of a language and also some alterations taking place in it, we can trace in any human group an adherence to traditions of language as well as the will to adapt expression to circumstances.

In my efforts to understand the spirit of a language, I worked as much on the structure of the language as on the literature or philosophy of the group using it. They illumine each other and together provide the only real path to true acquaintance. The users of a language are generally unaware of how they use it and how its structure affects their own thinking, sometimes preventing them from entering into a real contact with other human beings.

It may be worthwhile for every language learner to stop for a moment and consider whether the difficulties experienced in uttering sounds of another language, with a throat that in babyhood could produce any sounds, are not an example of how a mental process gets hold of a somatic mechanism and makes it rigid. Is it not possible that the practice of one language affects similarly the working of the mind, making it so rigid that we believe only in what can be expressed in that language and appear slightly paralyzed when using another? Anyone who has listened to school children using a foreign language taught to them via translation knows that one's own language is an obstacle to the understanding of texts in the other, as well as in the utterance of the simplest statements in the foreign language.

From outside, one could say that it is the different structures of languages that cause the insecurity, and that if one knew enough of the foreign grammar, and had a sufficiently wide vocabulary, all would be well. This unfortunately is not the case. Grammar is not of much help, nor even is a rich vocabulary. Only when one is really imbued with the literature or soaked in the environment of the people using the language can one express oneself in speech or writing as a native would. It is the spirit of a language that has to get hold of one's mind and dictate the expressions that sound right and fully convey the meaning to native listeners or readers. To be "English," a text does not only have to show English words or English sentences; it must convey those characteristics of the language which are acquired unconsciously and as a result of molding which takes place during years of living in an environment where English is spontaneously used. The way of saying anything in a particular language involves tacit agreements

20

which completely exclude the appearance of certain words which are most natural in another language. For example, for key words, the English prefer verbs and the French nouns. French speakers make nouns out of most adjectives, the English make verbs out of them. Ambiguity is hateful to the French, but is quite acceptable to the English. Context is for the French made of a set of statements and is equivalent to them, but it is additional for the English and it is allowed to affect the meaning of each sentence.

If all this is true, then where does the spirit of a language lie? Must we study all the expressions and the philosophy of any people whose language we want to learn before we can hope to reach a good mastery of it? Provisionally, the answer is "yes". For it would be a mistake to continue to believe that grammars and vocabularies are the keys to the proper use of languages. One often meets scholars with a good command of a language who are still shy when using it with the natives. This is only because they are not confident that the most adequate word will spontaneously present itself to provide the best expression, the one a native speaker would use. This would not be the case if they were as much at home with one language as with the other.

In fact, the spirit of each language can be reached in a number of ways. More than one way may be needed to supply the proper knowledge of it.

Since the spirit of a language is accessible to children who live in the environment, and who learn their mother tongue by hearing it first and using it later, it seems a good guess that something of its spirit lies in its melody. This means the particular effect of the flow of words upon one's flesh through the ears, the brain and the muscles. Once the melody is acquired, the process is reversed and utterance is through the conjunction of muscles, brain and flesh in general, checked by the ears as censors.

21

It is of interest here to mention the relationship of our flesh to music being heard. The true listener yields to the complexes that we call music and is actually affected by it to the point where all parts of his body can indicate its presence.* The listener who interferes by his imagery, his thoughts or by closing his sensitivity does not show the presence of the music in his flesh.

Since babies learn to talk their mother tongue first by yielding to its "music," I think that we can trace the first elements of the spirit of a language to the unconscious surrender of our sensitivity to what is conveyed by the background of noise in each language. This background obviously includes the silences, the pauses, the flow, the linkages of words, the duration of each breath required to utter connected chunks of the language, the overtones and undertones, the stresses as well as the special vowels or consonants belonging to that language.

Each language is distinctive in that respect.

We have, therefore, found one way to connect ourselves with the spirit of a language. This can at once become a technique if we set out, for instance, to acquire the capacity of surrendering to the sounds of recordings of native chatter before we attempt to analyze these sounds or to utter them ourselves. Surrender to the melody of a language, as to music, will bring to our unconscious all of the spirit of a language that has been stored in the melody. It cannot be reached otherwise. *Surrender is a technique for learning languages.* Only those who undertake such exercises can comment on its validity. It may not be easy, and it may not agree with everyone. I still believe that it is one of the important gates to re-sensitizing ourselves to what we were already sensitive to when learning our mother tongue. This, unfortunately, is left out as a technique by intellectualist approaches.

*cf. *Un nouveau phénomène psychosomatique*, C. Gattegno and A. Gay, Delachaux et Niestle, 1952, Neuchâtel and Paris.

But languages are also something other than their background of noises. Is there another component that characterizes their spirit?

Structure is a word currently used by linguists.

Do languages have as distinctive structures as they have melodies? The answer seems to be "yes."

If we take languages that belong to vastly different ethnic groups, it is easy to recognize that they use equivalent words in different places. But if we take languages from the same groups, they often keep corresponding words in corresponding places. Yet learners who try to learn another language to a reasonable level of competence find it as hard to acquire a similar as a dissimilar language. If structure, in this sense the set of empty places to be filled by words with different grammatical functions, were a characterisitic of the spirit of a language, grammar would provide an entry into it and I do not believe that it does.

But if we consider structure as being the set of expressions (including words as a special case) that can be connected in sequences to provide meanings more adequately, we can see that each language handles these connections in distinctly different ways, corresponding to its philosophical requirements and the spirit of the group's tradition.

It seems legitimate to consider that words, in so far as they contribute to the spirit of a language, are of two kinds: those that simply need substitution one for another to convey their meaning in whatever other language they are uttered, and those that cannot be dealt with in this way. The first kind includes all names of objects that belong to the environments of the peoples using the languages in question; most nouns are in this category. These words can be matched by one-to-one correspondences, and we could conceive of them as being in vocabularies. They can be either recalled or looked up when needed.

23

The second category of words is the one that generates the problems in language learning for translators, for analysts, philologists and linguists. Since it is not possible to resort to a one-to-one correspondence, the only way open is to reach the area of meaning which the words cover, and to find in oneself whether this is a new experience which yields something of the spirit of the new language, or whether there is an equivalent experience expressed differently in one's own. All translators know this problem well. Readers will understand it at once if they consider what happens to them when they are exposed to texts in the various disciplines of the arts or sciences which use as the medium of expression words of their mother tongue. Some are completely closed books requiring not only a capacity to decipher words, but also training, hard work, and often a new sensitivity which will give meaning to what we hear and read. What we concede easily in this case, we find most difficult to concede when we consider another language. Most of us believe that if we knew the vocabulary and the syntax we would understand any text in that language that deals with everyday experiences. My contention is that this belief is not based upon facts; that to make sense of an original text written by a native, one needs much more than a morphological knowledge of the language and the possession of a set of equivalents for words.

The greatest difficulty I experienced, and still do, with English is in the correct use of prepositions and of some tenses, about which I believe I know a great deal intellectually. The whole of myself protested at the denial of the right in English to use the future tense after "when" where the future was involved in the meaning; and at using expressions like "looking forward *to seeing you*" instead of *"to see you"*, which conveyed *to me* the true meaning, and much better. Such strange uses of the language are common among learners who choose to be at peace within themselves rather than bow to the traditions of the foreign language, even if they are mistaken grammatically.

Natives on the whole do not know what the spirit of their own language is, precisely because in acquiring it they have, on the one hand, developed a mode of thought which they eventually conceive of as *the* way of thinking; and, on the other hand, they experience — but without becoming aware of it — a reduction of their sensitivity, which they are shocked to discover when confronted with a foreign language. The word "foreign" does not help matters either. Most people do not feel that there is really any point in acquiring another language for what it *does* to oneself rather than for what it *brings* to one.

If it is true that we blunt our sensitivities by the mere process of acquiring our mother tongue, developing a special way of being while we acquire it, we can then see how important it is to think of language learning as a recovery of the innocence of our self, as a return to our full powers and our full potentials.

It can easily be seen that we can achieve this only by rejecting the learning of vocabularies and grammar and by replacing it with as thorough a penetration of the spirit of a language as possible. Methods of teaching to this end are needed, and the one considered in this book has been devised for that purpose. The following chapters will give an idea of how it can be achieved more easily than it would *a priori* appear here.

Outwardly, languages still remain sets of words which are used to make sentences according to certain rules described in grammars. Words are classified as nouns, verbs, pronouns, adverbs, adjectives, etc., in all languages. It is conceivable that a selection of the patterns of phrases and sentences can be presented to learners, who memorize them and then find, in a vocabulary list, the words that could replace certain others, while leaving the pattern untouched. One would, in a way, be "learning" the language by practicing its patterns with its vocabulary. Millions have actually "learned" languages in that way, and their success proves that the belief of its advocates has a correct foundation.

And yet, is there not in the consciousness of the users of languages learned in that way a veil which indicates that their sensitivity is still unaffected by the consumption of time taken to reach the knowledge that they have? Does not this absence of sensitivity reappear in the lack of confidence of such learners when confronted with certain uses of the languages they have learned.

On the other hand, there are examples of people who would appear to the natives as one of themselves until a gross mistake betrays that they have not practiced the language for as long as native speakers have and to the extent that is normal for the natives at the age of the user.

The first, in contrast to the second, have not surrendered to the spirit of the language and have concentrated upon forms *per se*, leaving to chance the conveyance of whatever of the spirit can be found in practicing the molds *per se*. The second have reached the keys of the non-verbal parts of language and they use them to convey meaning beyond, and in addition to, words and structures.

It seems to me that the practice of breathing in a certain way, and the use and practice of what I want to call the *functional* vocabulary will, to a certain extent, provide classroom equivalents of what is picked up naturally in an environment where the language is normally spoken.

Though it is obvious to all of us that we speak our own tongue differently when we are relaxed or tired, out of breath or in control of our flow of words, it rarely occurs to linguists to consider whether some languages present special features because of the demands they normally make on the pneumatic systems of their users. A language like English, in which so many short words are commonly used, gives much more often than German the occasion for short pauses, thus making the English more inclined to speak slowly and mutedly, and the Germans more inclined to embark with vigor upon what sounds like a speech on the most ordinary matter. This is inevitable because of their way of describing things by linking a number of words into one. Because Germans place a key word, their verb, at the end of a sentence, no matter how many clauses are inserted in it, German speakers tend to race to the end of every statement to convey their meaning. The breathing requirements of their language are thus different from those of English.

So the spirit of a language can be reached still better if learners are made aware of the breathing requirements of different languages. This meets the melodic component somewhere, since the line of a melody, as distinct from its notes, is concerned with time factors, which in turn are connected with the qualities of breathing if the voice is the instrument or part of it.

This has been a very brief and sketchy consideration of breathing as a way to the spirit of languages. To discuss it in greater detail would take us too far in a book of this kind, though I believe the problem to be of fundamental importance.

We are left with one more avenue to the spirit of a language: its functional vocabulary, which we define as that part of the language which cannot be fully conveyed by a one-to-one correspondence of words. Nouns in some languages have two or three genders, adjectives in some are variable, in others invariable; variability also occurs in the position of words, in the cases according to meaning or historical development of the language, with regard to exceptions, etc. If we can meet all these as natural linguistic behavior, and never use comparison with our mother tongue to contrast and judge them as oddities, we shall let the language form its corresponding mental structures in our minds. These structures will respond as readily as do the earlier ones formed during infancy, if they come with their criteria built in, and not through a deferred activity that will slow down the whole process and make the use of the new language strange and different from what, through the experience with the mother tongue, one understands by use of a language.

If it were possible to practice the multivalent forms or molds of language while making sense of the statements, and to meet as verbal equivalents of simple situations statements that directly convey what the eyes perceived, then the relation of words to one's mind would be not through memorization and translation, but through the well-practiced mechanism of associating sounds with what one experiences. Since meanings are not reducible to the set of words in sentences, if we relate sounds directly to meanings we have provided integrative schemata that will hold the sounds together as they are met, and will not require the effort of association which usually accompanies memory.

The *rightness* of a statement is to be felt, not deduced. Deduction may be needed when spontaneous means fail. If we have made proper use of the melody of the language, the rightness of any statement that is made of words, and not only of hummed sounds, results from the coincidence of the recognition of structure and of melody. A right enunciation of a sequence of noises would give the impression that it is of a given language even if it did not contain a single word from that language.

The *correctness* of a statement lies in the matching of the sequence of words with the required habits of the natives making such statements. A correct statement may be followed by a wrong consequence if the words do not refer to what one has in mind, so that correctness is a necessary condition for adequacy, but it is not sufficient — just as a right statement may altogether escape the criteria of correctness and adequacy for want of any verbal support to carry analytic meaning.

The *adequacy* of a statement results from a matching of what is evoked by the words with the supporting dimensions (perceptive and active) of the corresponding situation.

If we wish to maintain the integration of the three criteria as it exists in the spontaneous use of a language by natives, we must practice rightness through the ear, correctness through practice in specific situations, and adequacy through actions in those situations. It is not necessary to use the whole of the language for that, nor even to suggest that patterns are often met and are thus the recurrent part of the language which should be practiced. It is enough to develop means that will give the learner facilities to form inner criteria that operate spontaneously and which will later on be extended to include ever-widening chunks of the language. (This extension will require separate attention, as it is a function of general experience and not of training in the language alone.)

To close this chapter, it may be helpful to study further the notion of *inner criteria*, which play such an important part in one's education throughout all of one's life, and seem neglected by the majority of educators in schools.

It is today common in engineering to reserve a part of the energy used by any piece of machinery to indicate that it is functioning well, and to act upon the flow of energy through it so as to keep it working according to the program. A similar control mechanism has been found in our bodies, controlling physiological phenomena in order to maintain health. It has been sought in the brain, but no one has undertaken to find whether it also exists in psychological phenomena. Still, it does not even take a moment to discover that most of us know at once whether we have just uttered a word that is unwanted or out of

29

sequence, or whether we have distorted a sound. We immediately provide the alternative wanted. This proves that while we are engaged in the jobs of talking, writing, discussing, etc., part of our consciousness is occupied in supervising the activity. This part feeds back to the self in charge information which is used at once to either let the flow go on or to introduce corrections where needed, in order to make the objective material which has been produced comply with the schema that pre-existed and provoked the activity.

These sets of criteria are obviously in the mind and have never been seen as objects, though one may think of them in a moment of imagination as links between neurons in the brain, or else as habits, when one loses interest in probing any further. In order not to mortgage research, we will vaguely call them inner criteria. Like all psychic material, their existence is of a type which is immaterial for the moment but nonetheless real, as one can easily convince oneself psychically by asking, for example, what it means to know that one really understands the statement: "I can write blue with white chalk."

All immediately functioning criteria must already be in the mind to act as soon as an opportunity arises. But these criteria may not have been there always in one's life. They could have been produced by the mind at a certain stage when producing other mental material, such as mental structures. It is obvious to any observer of babies that they do not possess all the criteria they will possess later on. Hence, these are the outcome of deliberate work on one's mind at different moments in the continuum of time.

While machines only work after they have been completed, lubricated and endowed with energy, mental structures, because they are temporal in essence, function at all stages but change themselves while working, integrating new material, removing some other and becoming very different in function and purpose when of a certain size.

30

This fascinating elaboration of our mental structures is with us all the time throughout life and could have been known to everyone of us if we were only concerned with it. Yet it still remains mysterious, and is even denied existence by most teachers and psychologists in their work with learners. The process of producing mental structures takes care of itself, and the criteria of rightness, correctness and adequacy are developed as we go along, not at the end of learning or at a given moment (unless the end is every moment, which is the correct way of looking at the continuum of time). So, for me, everything produced by the mind at work while objectifying mental energy into mental structures is psychologically correct, even though outwardly, socially, it is not yet what it will be later on when the criteria are formed and used to transform the material until it becomes adequate. That is why in my approach I do not correct learners; I only throw them back onto themselves to elaborate further their criteria and to use them more completely. Against a common teachers' demand for immediate correctness through so-called imitation, I take upon myself the burden of controlling myself so as not to interfere. By doing so I give time to a student to make sense of "mistakes," (which are precious indicators of the discrepancy between what is and what should be) and to develop exercises that foster progress.

It is simply because I am aware that only self-education will lead any learner to the mastery of a skill, and because I found in my own learning a multiplicity of obstacles that needed dealing with separately and in original ways, that I was able to develop the silent way of teaching, in which the learner matters most.

To require perfection at once is the great imperfection of most teaching and most thinking about teaching. Since we can only obtain approximation of the goal from people moving towards it, we must develop techniques of teaching that are molded onto reality and take into account what is

31

going on in the learners all the time. No true domination of any field is possible without exploration of it, and this depends upon existing means; but it also suggests the means needed to pursue it. It is this double movement of the mind that we have neglected so badly in our teaching of all subjects. It can be restored if we realize that the return to the core of knowledge already consolidated is a necessary step for integration and the formation of criteria which then permit bigger jumps ahead. Readers can be helped to see this more clearly through the analogy of the increase of the volume of muscles that results from practice, and if they think of the existence of developed muscles as the power to do things which were impossible to attempt earlier.

Without immediate inner criteria functioning well, no true learning of language is possible beyond a certain point. With them, we can expect that what seemed the privilege of the exceptionally gifted is indeed open to all, just as it has been open to all to learn the mother tongue.

Inner criteria should be nurtured by teachers, who will find that time spent in establishing them is no waste but serves to introduce the very valuable concept of the cumulative effect of learning, which replaces the linear pattern of the acquisition of language by an exponential one. (That is, it replaces equal "amounts" for equal durations by larger and larger "amounts" for equal durations as we move forward.) What seems in the beginning a slow pace will soon become a fast movement forward that was never envisaged in the classroom, though it is obvious in young children learning to talk.

In the next chapter, I describe in some detail how we go about establishing inner criteria in the learners. But the best way of finding out about it is to observe learners and reflect upon what they are doing, how and why. Here, too, self-education is the only education, and this applies to the teacher who wants to know what it really is to learn a foreign language.

a u i e o e o   ´ ` ·
ha u i   ho   h
    w y

---

n l s s t m d p v r f b n x

c c sc g g gl gn qu z z
ch ci sci gh gi gli cqu

3.

Much Language and Little Vocabulary

This will be a summarized exposition of what I believe we can achieve with the techniques that put into practice what has been discussed in the previous two chapters.

The title of this chapter has already indicated that it is possible to make a distinction between language and vocabulary. I claim that we can teach much language although we limit considerably the amount of vocabulary.

Let us imagine that we are looking at a class of interested students of any age (6 or 11 or 14 or adults), and that the teacher enters the room for the first time. The class knows that it will study a foreign language, and the teacher is determined not to use one single word of the vernacular, which he may know, or which may even be his mother tongue.

The approach is, as I have insisted, most artificial. The box of colored rods that the teacher places on his desk is all he carries. He opens it and draws out of it one rod and shows it to the class while saying in the foreign language the word for rod, with the indefinite article if it exists in that language. He puts it down in silence and picks up another of a different color and says the same (one or two) words again, and so on, going through seven or eight rods and never asking for anything. The intrigued students have attentively noted the events and heard some noises which to them will seem the same while their eyes see only different objects and a repetition of the same action. Without any fuss the teacher then lifts a rod and asks in mime for the sounds he uttered. Bewildered, the class would not respond, in general, but the teacher says "a rod" and asks again in mime for another effort from the class. Invariably someone guesses (perhaps from the habits ingrained in traditional teaching) that the teacher wants back what he gave. When in his own way the pupil says something approximating what the teacher said, the teacher may smile or nod, showing how content he is at being understood. At the next trial almost the whole class repeats the sounds for a rod (very approximately in most cases). The teacher does not inquire whether some students are thinking of a piece of wood, others of lifting something, or something different. Contact has been established without the vernacular, and that is all that was wanted so far.

The teacher then introduces the names for four or five of the colors, giving the sounds for "a blue rod," "a black rod," "a red rod," "a yellow rod," "a green rod" or any other combination of the ten colors available. Because the names of the colors are now added the pupils can no longer imagine that different expressions mean the same action and are forced to conclude that the teacher is giving the phrases that summarily describe these objects. The exercise is now shifted to practice in uttering the foreign sounds for the six or seven objects, so that as soon as one rod replaces another, one utterance replaces another, which would be the case in the vernacular.

This may be the end of the first lesson. Usually it is not and the teacher motions two pupils to come and stand near him. He turns to one and says in the foreign language: "take a blue rod." (He has previously made sure that the set of rods on which this action is to be performed has more than one rod of each color.) Naturally, no response is to be expected, except perhaps the utterance of the words for "a blue rod." So the teacher says the words again while putting the pupil's hand over the set and making his fingers take a blue rod from the pile. Then he says: "take a brown rod" or "take a yellow rod," etc., and can expect a correct action as a response. He does this a number of times, for it is natural that while the pupil is concentrating on choosing the correct rod he does not produce the substitute in his own mind for the word "take." The teacher then turns to the other student and does what he did before but fewer times. Then dramatically he changes places with one of the students and indicates that the student should now utter the words first. Someone in the class usually gets the idea. If not, the teacher goes back to the previous situation and does what he did before once or twice again. The exchange of places this time yields the required results: the equivalent of "take a blue (or red . . .) rod" is uttered by one or the other of the students. When the teacher complies with this, he is conveying an agreement that the rules of the game are being observed.

The next lesson usually shows that the time separating the two sessions has served the students well. The quick revision of the sounds for the names of the colored rods proves that the class pronounces them on the whole much better than the previous time.

Calling two other students, the teacher says: "take . . . .," and the action is performed at once, usually correctly. But this time the teacher adds: "give it to me," and indicates with his hand that he wants it. As he does it with different rods and alternately with each of the two students, the set of noises for "give it to me" is put into circulation. Then, after saying "take a . . . ," the teacher says: "give it to him" (or "her", according to the sex of the student and the demands of a particular language), and indicates that this time it is to be given to the other student (the teacher may have to use his hands to convey the meaning).

The class has heard phrases and sentences being used from the start by a number of students, or even all of them, more or less adequately, but at least approximately recognizably. The language covered is: a rod, a yellow, red, blue . . . rod, take a . . . rod, give it to him, her, me.

What is significant is that the set of rods has helped:

● To avoid the vernacular.

● To create simple linguistic situations that are under the complete control of the teacher.

● To pass on to the learners the responsibility for the utterance of the descriptions of the objects shown or the actions performed.

● To let the teacher concentrate on what the students say and how they are saying it, drawing their attention to the differences in pronunciation and the flow of words.

● To generate a serious gamelike situation in which the rules are implicitly agreed upon by giving meaning to the gestures of the teacher and his mime.

● To permit almost from the start a switch from the lone voice of the teacher using the foreign language to a number of voices using it. This introduces components of pitch, timbre, intensity that will constantly reduce the impact of one voice and hence reduce imitation and encourage personal production of one's own brand of the sounds.

● To provide the support of perception and action to the intellectual guess of what the noises may mean, thus bringing in the arsenal of the usual criteria of experience already developed and automatic in one's use of the mother tongue.

• To provide durations of spontaneous speech upon which the teacher and the students can work to obtain a similarity of melody to the one heard, thus providing melodic integrative schemata from the start.

In the first few lessons this will be deliberate, but will soon become a framework of conventional handling of this teaching. The students will be astonished to find that their teacher stands through much of the lessons, that he keeps them concentrating all the time, that he says less and less and they more and more, that he neither approves nor disapproves but throws them back upon their own tools of judgment, indicating that they must listen better, use their mouths differently, stress here or there, shorten one sound and prolong another. Very soon, the more or less arbitrary conventions he introduces become accepted between himself and his class.

In four or five lessons the vocabulary will have increased very little. The *plurals* of "rod", of the *adjectives* (if they exist) and of the *pronouns* are introduced, plus the *conjunction* "and"; some *possessive adjectives* and perhaps one or two demonstrative ones. The *numerals* "one", "two" and perhaps "three" are added — generally there may be about thirty words in circulation.

These are: one noun: *rod*; color adjectives: *red, green, yellow, black, brown, blue*; numeral adjectives: *one, two, three*; articles: *a* and *the* (of one gender or neutral only, in languages that require them); verbs in the imperative: *take, give* and, perhaps, *put*; personal pronouns: *me, him, her, it, them*; possessive adjectives: *his, her, my*; the adverbs: *here, there*; the preposition: *to*; the conjunction: *and* — or 27 words.

But with them we have heard and understood, and uttered and understood:

take a ——— rod (six or seven colors)

give it to ——— (him, her, me)

and their conjunctions:

take a ——— rod and give it to ———

or: take ——— rods and give them to ——— .

These produce a large number of sentences. Obviously, there are hundreds of different utterances possible, though the general impression is that the number is much smaller because the changes between one phrase and the next may be of only one word. More utterances are easily found if we use the conjunctions as well:

take a ——— rod and a ——— rod and give them to ——— . . . , and even longer ones.

The importance of this exercise is that it allows us to work on the formation of a natural way of using the melody of the foreign language. This allows the learners to gain from the start something of the spirit of the language that is usually left for much later in linguistic studies.

It is my contention that we are giving our students something of great value by restricting the vocabulary but extending as much as we can the length of the statements uttered with ease, and in the way one uses one's own language.

Since the way we breathe has a cultural component, and since uttering statements is connected with breathing, we can see why we will be gaining more and more of the spirit of the language as we learn to alter our breathing to suit its melody.

For the teacher, the technique is a conscious way of affecting his students' unconscious relation to this new speech. As a result of it, the students will gain what cannot be passed on by explanation but can be reached by intuition and the surrender to the traditions absorbed in the spirit of a particular language.

39

To reinforce this awareness, the use of the discs or tapes can be invaluable. The question put implicitly to the class is: "Which of the speeches you hear is the language we have been studying?" There is no question of the students' understanding the meaning of the words used on the record, but if they can distinguish the one they are meeting in class from others as well as from their mother tongue, we must agree that their ear has been sensitized to the recognition of something that is part of each language but outside the vocabulary: this, I repeat, is part of the spirit of a language.

To further reinforce this awareness, we use a new tool and a new technique. This tool is our set of wallcharts, on which are printed in colors the words we have learned so far. Whether or not the script of the foreign language is familiar to the learner will make a slight difference. We will proceed in our argument without considering that point here, but we will do so briefly later in this discussion.

We will use only Wallchart No. 1 first.* On it are printed at random all the 27 words which have been learned plus a few more according to the demands of the language studied, one exception being that the first words are "a rod" (or "rod"). Using a long pointer, the teacher points at words, one by one, asking the class to say them (this no longer requires his saying the words since the previous games have established the convention). When in doubt about the ability of some of the students to do it, he asks individuals to say the words on their own. In this way, the teacher can find out whether the learners recognize the printed equivalents of the oral words they have met in factual situations with the rods.

Once he is sure of this, the teacher links words, using the pointer, with the convention that if it points at one word followed by a pause (at which time the pointer is no

*See Figure I.

40

longer pointing at a word), that word is uttered alone; if it points at two or more words in succession, all these words must be uttered and in that order. This convention is established in no time. Clearly, the teacher is silent during all the movements of the pointer and afterwards, when turning to the students and waiting for a volunteer or volunteers to utter the phrase or sentence. When the class can sufficiently well utter these words in succession, the speed of pointing can be varied so that the convention of the speed of flow of words is brought in again. We call this exercise *Visual Dictation.*

This new technique is extremely powerful in that now the learner's mind is still more in contact with his own self. Moreover, visual imagery is brought in without any fuss or lengthy preparation, and it sustains the words heard in the foreign language as it already does in the mother tongue. Because visual images are swift and have extension and depth, they will give the learners new powers not contained in temporal sequences. In heard and uttered sentences, the temporal sequence is linear, that is, it is not reversible without real alteration of the sequence. With the chart in front of the pupils the words are all *seen* simultaneously, and contain a large number of possible choices of subsets that can be objectified by the convention of moving the pointer to create links between words. Until now, actions and perception have commanded the utterances, which were thus linked with the language and integrated as a result of the active lessons; but from now on, since it is known that words pointed at suggest noises to be made, any sequence of noises can be generated — nonsense statements as well as rational ones, including the ones that have been mastered. Here, therefore, is a new way of producing statements by simply selecting some of the words on the charts, thus giving rise to exercises that can serve new ends and test mastery of certain parts of the language.

If the teacher shows, for example, "Give me a blue rod", the pupils can obviously say it, but it is not at all certain that they will understand the meaning, since so far they have only been told in certain definite circumstances which no longer obtain: "Give it to me". Nevertheless, if someone came to the table, took a blue rod and gave it to the teacher, no one would doubt that he had made sense of the new sequence of words. If no one can do it, all that has been gained so far is an ability to use the chart to produce sequences of sounds with a certain intonation, at a certain speed — which indicates some acquaintance with the melody of the language. This is not negligible.

As this silent exercise goes on, the teacher can increase the number of words pointed at, he can show them with quicker and quicker movements of the pointer and at the end get the whole statement from some pupils. Is it a small thing to have students of seven or eleven who do not know much of the language breathe out, with a command of diction that is quite acceptable, a sentence of the following length? — "Take a blue rod and a green rod and give her the blue one and give him the green one."

If we have succeeded in establishing the rule that the sequence selected will be shown only once, the success of this exercise is a clear indication that the learners are now capable of behaving somehow as native speakers with respect to their breathing and their association of sound and sign. Students who can achieve such feats after so few lessons are teaching us that they can easily be taken much further than we have ever believed possible.

Visual Dictation is a twofold technique in which the teacher points at words and the students say what was shown, or the students find the words on the charts after the teacher has uttered a whole sentence. This second exercise will easily be changed into oral dictation, in which a full sentence is said and the learners write it down. If all the vocabulary contained in the sentence is covered by the charts, there are two stages in this oral dictation. In one, the learners can look up at the charts to find any word they cannot write: in the other, it is agreed not to look at the charts, or these are removed.

Before pursuing this matter, let us consider the case of a foreign language whose script is entirely alien to the learners, which uses different shapes, different conventions for their formation, and their alignment on paper. There are many such cases among the languages of the world: some people write from left to right, others from right to left, some above, others below the line, others vertically instead of horizontally; some use characters that are difficult to disentangle (as are the Chinese or Japanese ideograms), others use signs for whole syllables, or additional conventions that represent tone, etc. The writer's experiments have been only with some of these, and his conclusions may not be universally valid. Still, for what they are, it is a fact that there has never been need to introduce the writing conventions as such, but simply to make the writing follow the oral exercises and to associate noises already met with signs now introduced. No difference has been noted between peoples using the same script to represent different sounds (as, for example, for English and Spanish) and peoples using very different conventions (as in the case of Israelis who meet English for the first time, after being accustomed to a different script, when they write from right to left and do not write their vowels; or Amharas learning French, while their own characters are different, number 251, and are syllables and not letters). The learners could even recognize in the written speech conventions that were not pointed out to them, and used the clues to decipher written words that they had never yet heard. For example, while teaching Hindi to users of the Latin alphabet who had never seen Sanskrit letters, I wrote a sentence meaning "Take a yellow rod and give it to me." Then I showed the class which word was "give." This clue was sufficient for a Champollionesque deciphering of the whole sentence, and the formation of a list of signs whose associated sounds were ascertained by cross-reference and by my silent acceptance of the solution. A number of words was then added and read correctly, though no sound was uttered for them by me.

This indicates that students have all the necessary equipment to meet the challenges presented, and that it is unnecessary to give special lessons to introduce the letters or characters of the foreign language as long as a sufficient number of clues is provided. In this approach, the clues are that part of the spoken language that has already been mastered and used. It is preferable when a new script is presented not to show a chart, but to write first on the board, step by step, the words that will become the content of the first chart. No colored chalks are necessary in my experience, but if they are available they can be used with better results.

Let us stress that the introduction of the written word can be postponed until the teacher feels that it will make the greatest contribution. It has not yet been clearly established whether the fifth or tenth or thirtieth lesson is the most appropriate time for it. Each teacher will learn by trial and error, mainly by error.

It is to be understood that an approach like this one, based as it is on awareness and on personal responsibility for learning, cannot be conceived as rigid. In order to help as much as I could in the direction of flexibility, I have included in the first few charts words of the functional vocabulary that could form groups of lessons in some degree independent of each other. The teachers can work around one or the other group according to taste, circumstances and personal philosophy.

Of special interest is the Numerals Chart. It contains the words for the numerals 1, 2, 3, 4 and so on, that one needs in order to be able to read and say any number of any length. The various languages we publish require a different set of words, since the various cultures have developed their own description of number. 83 is *eighty-three* in English, *drei und achtzig* in German, *quatre-vingt-trois* in French, *ochenta y tres* in Spanish, etc. But with about 30 words, we can form as many number names as we wish. The pointer and this chart can, in a lesson or little more, provide experience in naming all numbers. Let us describe its use for the English language.

The words, arranged at random and printed in the color-code are: *one, two, three ... ten, eleven, twelve, thirteen, fifteen, —teen, twenty, thirty, forty, fifty, —ty, eighty, hundred, thousand, million, a, and*: 26 words or signs.

The teacher has already used the rods to teach the first few numerals, and the students know how to count in their own language, but the younger students may not necessarily know how to read long strings of figures. Using the pointer, the teacher gets the class to say, in chorus, each word on the chart following the sequence 1, 2, 3. . . . When he reaches sixteen, he forms it by sliding the pointer to join *six* and *—teen*, when he reaches *twenty-one*, he joins *twenty* and *one*, thus showing that the pointer is used here to produce the name of one entity: a numeral. The analysis of its component parts is imposed upon the learner as it is on the native speakers. He must accept it as a convention if he wants to play this game. As we advance in the sequence of numerals, the numeration rules are made evident, so that we acquire the power to form millions of sounds in different combinations for millions of distinct entities. Long names of numerals provide not only exercises in elocution, breathing and melody in the foreign language, but also an intellectual exercise. For it is permissible to use the pointer to join a number of the words on the chart and ask the learners to write the corresponding figures; we can ask the class to read it and have one of the students point out on the chart the corresponding component words. When he is mistaken, he is corrected by others. It is clear that it is not necessary to know how to read numerals in one's own language in order to carry out this exercise correctly in the new one. This exercise can, in a short time, provide the mastery of reading numerals in a new language even if it is not yet available in the mother tongue. More than a new capacity is acquired here. The new language has gained the positive emotional value of having served to increase one's insight into one's own language. This contribution is made so early in the study of the new language that it is worth mentioning here. Usually one expects such results only from much wider knowledge and from a prolonged acquaintance with a foreign language. The use of the Numerals Chart is a good example of how with little vocabulary we can generate much language, since we have now potentially produced an infinite set of words in the foreign language to describe an infinite set of objects that exist, like all other objects, outside of languages. Students do feel that when this chart and its various uses have been mastered they have made a big step forward. This feeling is a positive ally that will assist progress and increase the speed of learning, the depth of awareness and familiarity with the language. It is easy to imagine that, if two or three weeks after starting the study of a foreign language children or adults can say the name of a number as long as 3,644,572,893,608, they legitimately feel that their mind and body are at par with those of native speakers. In fact, in this field, they have no reason to envy the ordinary users of that language. They have achieved the maximum; it is within themselves, and they can have recourse to it if they wish to feel the language, its melody and its requirements upon their breathing. Since numerals form a "closed experience" on the linguistic plane, it seems sensible to introduce them early and gain all that their study can contribute: it is much more than one would ever be able to do with an equal number of words of any other category (names or colors, for example,) that cannot produce meaning by being strung together. The Numerals Chart is a veritable mine for our purposes in this approach.

Each one of the charts will extend the powers of the learners, for they will find in it a set of words that will permit them to talk and write about relationships that occur constantly in life.

Some of the charts are linked with experiences other than the ones considered so far but which can still be described with the rods. Spatial relations such as being between, above, next to, perpendicular to, parallel to, across, on top, in front, etc., can be studied with their reciprocity or dissymmetry. *Larger than* does not reverse except to *smaller than*, while *parallel to* is a reciprocal relationship. *Between* A and B is equivalent to *between* B and A, but B *bigger than* A and *smaller than* C becomes A *smaller than* B and C. These variations on the theme are an obvious source of much language, but are based upon perception and describing with very few words all that can be said within one situation.

The comparative and the superlative of adjectives are, in the case of some obvious attributes, well practised with the rods and easily transferred to the charts and Visual Dictation.

Temporal relationships can be exemplified by actions in which the rods only play the role of objects that can be introduced in situations but they could have been replaced by different ones. *After, before, successively, slowly, quickly, alternately, first, second, then, with, at the same time as, intermittently, simultaneously, while*, etc., are easily illustrated by situations produced especially for that purpose. Tenses too can be brought in by the same means, first orally, in situations, then by

47

forming sentences with the pointer and words on the charts.

We must include in the functional vocabulary the forms of irregular verbs as well as the conjugation of most usual verbs. It is well known that irregularity in languages comes from use: the more words are used, the more they wear out, and this is shown in their irregularities. So the most often used words will require special study, but they will appear often enough in statements not to demand a special effort of memory.

On the charts are included the various forms of the irregular verbs that are most common in the description of spatio-temporal situations. A number of exercises with the pointer will provide the oral practice necessary to establish sounds in the minds of the learners. Whenever possible, situations will be generated to illustrate some of these forms. The remainder of the forms can be learned on the charts, since otherwise it would mean that true transfer of knowledge from words to general experience has not taken place and that work on previous situations is still required.

We see in the list of words on the charts that the words for box, for the lid of the box, color, length, top, end, and side are included. These are obviously not "functional", but because of their small number they will not create a problem. On the contrary, they are essential for meaningful use of the whole functional vocabulary: they will, for example, give experience of noun-genders if these exist in the language.

Excluded from our charts are proper nouns or names though they may have been used extensively in the class. This justifies the use of the personal pronouns in the first charts.

It is obvious that very soon both the use of the rods and of the charts with the pointer will become second nature, and that the learners will have understood what is the meaning of a controlled linguistic situation and what one can get from it. They will soon find that as soon as some words are put into circulation their area of application is definable and it often coincides with the same area in their mother tongue. They will meet the foreign language as a language, meant to be used for communication, with the possibilities and limitations of one's own. This is one of the additional virtues everyone would want to find in any language learning approach. Words can form sentences, but contradictory statements cannot be acceptable, even though they can be uttered. This is true for any language because the statements made in each are about reality, and it is this that commands acceptance or rejection. Even imagination has its logic, and fantasy does not mean nonsense. It is not difficult to say "a black white rod," but it seems impossible to figure what it is if no alteration is brought to the statement, for example by inserting "and" between "black" and "white", or some similar change. If the learner has any understanding of the words he has met, he will know, because of his general experience, that such strings of words are no more acceptable in the foreign language than in his own.

While it is hard to think of an actual situation that is contradictory, it is very easy to produce any number of contradictory statements by pointing the words on the charts, or with pen on paper. These can serve as tests of whether understanding of the meaning of words used in various situations exists to a sufficient degree. A statement may be grammatically correct but logically unacceptable: for example, "the largest of these rods are the smallest among them."

It now becomes clear that the work we do with our reduced number of words casts a net that would enclose almost as vast an area of experience as would the whole of the language, except for the details of special situations, which can be thought of as the spaces in the net.

The more we advance in the study of the charts, the less need will there be for detailed practice, since intelligence has a place in study and provides the generalizations, the transfers, the sense of exceptions, etc., that reduce the burdens upon memory. The way in which the charts are constructed will indicate that we have made use of the cumulative effect of learning. While in the beginning we give material that is to be used as units in their own right, later we present parts of words which can be involved in a number of words, perhaps with radically different meanings and certainly with varying meanings when connected with prefixes or suffixes. This enhancement of the challenges offered is a tribute to the increase of power in the learner, who now can tackle much harder tasks than in the earlier stages of his apprenticeship.

Everything we have discussed in this chapter is under the heading of a reduced vocabulary. But we must not convey the false idea that a restricted vocabulary is not wide. It will be seen from the contents of the first dozen charts that we are here considering a functional vocabulary of about 400 words, of which a few are not strictly functional, but are nouns introduced arbitrarily because of our choice of material. With 400 well-selected words, a large number of statements can be made. In practice, we will only make a small number to illustrate the use of the material for our end, which is acquisition of a language to a certain level of competence for different purposes (a visit, an examination, business, etc.).

In the next chapter, we will cross the threshold of the various vocabularies and enter the field which covers the whole of each language we want to study.

或	还	就	离	地
者	向	转	共	越
只	对	太	远	来
每	错	自	吧	近
因	但	己	极	非
为	如	假	当	常
所	果	使	更	去
以	可	即	除	怎

4.

The Conquest of Vocabulary

In following up what has been done so far, we can say that we will embark now upon little additional language and much vocabulary.

In the previous chapters, I have written about what seems to me to matter in language learning, and about how to start students in that work through new techniques and materials. Most people believe that language is for use, and so do I. But they also believe that, if one is to use language in proper contexts, nouns and special vocabularies are the words needed, not those that we have practiced so far.

I still hope that they will agree with me that the first few weeks spent in acquiring those attributes of language that maintain its integrity and at the same time enhance that of the learners were well spent. If I can make my students acquire special vocabularies as well, and in economical ways, we will satisfy the requirements of needs and rigor.

Let me first make one general remark. If we have agreed that there is one vocabulary better suited than another to convey the spirit of a language and to provide experience of the structures of that language, and if it justifies the name of functional vocabulary, then the rest of the vocabulary can be called *luxury vocabulary.* Because the way we have worked so far is economically sound, we can now afford luxuries, we can enjoy adding frills to our basic knowledge or can accumulate material that may some day be of use. In the traditional way of teaching, or in some of the reformed approaches, the question has rarely been asked whether one needs to reach a certain level of competence before one can afford to acquire the specialized vocabulary, needed for circumstances that may be less universal.

But even in the luxury vocabulary we must distinguish the really luxury from the *semi-luxury.* Both are special, but one is so special that only specialists need it. This already obtains in one's own language. Most people need the word "bone", but not so many need the names of the classified vertebrae from neck to hip. Most people can say a few words about their television set or the engine of their car, but only the specialists need the words for every part of their mechanisms. Clearly, the evolution of languages includes the addition and subtraction of luxury words that come into or go out of usage.

Let us put into the semi-luxury category the words we would need to get along with natives in the business of day-to-day life, which will include food, clothing, travel, family life, outings and the like, but not philosophical discussions, political arguments and sources of information (economic, military, diplomatic . . .), nor any of the specialized languages of professions and trades. All these will be grouped together as *luxury proper.* Let us remember that we are still working in classrooms in lands where the language taught is not that of the environment, for if it were,* we would have to make allowances for changes in our classification, agreeing for example to call political vocabulary a semi-luxury vocabulary.

Our subdivision into semi-luxury and luxury-proper will govern our timetable for the conquest of vocabulary in the classroom (in lessons and in the materials offered). We first conquer the part of the language that would serve us best if we were to visit a country where it is used, and only then do we attempt the conquest of the luxury proper.†

The means at our disposal include texts, pictures, transparencies (in isolation or in filmstrips), films, and radio and television programs.

Where the language is not phonetic, the last wallcharts contain luxury vocabulary words, mainly in order to give examples of the various spellings in that language. If these charts can be used for Visual Dictation, they will afford verbal situations after the vocabulary has been explained by one or other of the means available.

This chapter is mainly devoted to a summary of the material and some of its uses in classroom situations.

1. Use of *ad hoc* drawings and accompanying worksheets
2. Use of transparencies and accompanying worksheets
3. Use of films and television programs
4. Texts and accompanying worksheets
5. Anthologies

*For example, in the case of Immigrants' Schools.
†If the purpose were to help people to acquire the language of a specialized field, naturally the language of that field would no longer be considered as luxury.

Anyone who sets out to provide integrative schemata for the learning that one does will find that there is a difference between a temporal sequence which only at the end suggests the schema that integrates the whole, and a spatial display that "seems" to be perceived all at once, although it is in fact only scanned. Nevertheless, if we use as integrative schema a picture of any scene, there is a danger that it may offer at the same time and at the same visual level elements whose names may be too special. It is open to us to ignore them, but just as we would not ignore a clause in a spoken statement, since we think that the clause belongs to it, we may also be forcing minds in an illegitimate direction if we ignore any elements of the picture. The solution lies in preparing special material for the purpose in mind, and deliberately relating the purpose to the material in the instructions for its use.

We shall consider here two of the drawings designed for a definite extension of vocabulary: they are Numbers 8 and 9 in the series of twelve.

Number 8 shows seven members of a family dressed to go out. The father is wearing a black suit, and is holding a hat in his hand. The mother is dressed in blue, has a hat, and is carrying a large black handbag. None of the children are wearing hats. There are two girls and three boys. The eldest boy has long trousers, the other two shorts. One of the girls has long fair hair and the other short auburn hair; both have small handbags. The colors of their dresses are different. Two of the boys are dark haired and the other is fair. All the children have blue eyes, like their mother's, but their father's are grey.

The picture can be used in such a way that the functional vocabulary already met can be practiced in new situations, but the main aim is to introduce the following vocabulary in any language.

55

This is the ———— *family*. The *father*, the *mother*, their two *daughters* and three *sons*. The *girls' names* are . . . , the *boys'* names are . . . They are going out for a *walk*, or perhaps to *church* or for a *visit*. Mother's *dress* is . . . , her *hat* is . . . . Father's *suit* is . . . , his *hat* is . . . There are *buttons* on mother's dress: they are *made of glass*. Her *handbag* is large and new. Father's suit has three *pieces*: a *jacket*, a *vest* and a *pair* of *trousers*. In the *buttonhole* of his jacket there is a red rose. On mother's hat there are *feathers*. She also has *earrings* and *is wearing gloves*. The girls both have *tidy hair*. One has a *ribbon* in it and the other one is wearing a *hair-band*. Their *handbags* are small — there may be a *handkerchief* in each. Each girl has a *belt* at the *waist* of her dress and one has a *bracelet* on her right *wrist*, while the other has a *wristwatch* on her left *arm*. They too have gloves but they are holding them in their left *hands*. The *eldest* boy has a new suit. He has a *sweater* under his jacket and his two brothers each have one too: one *buttons up* in the middle, and the other has long *sleeves* that can be seen under his coat sleeves. The smallest boy has short hair, the eldest has his *parted* on the side, and the other has a *crew-cut*. They each have a *tie* of a different color. Father's is black. The *shoes* of all of them are *shining* — they have been *polished* with *care* just before *leaving*. It is not possible to see Father's *socks* nor those of the eldest boy, because of their trousers; but the other boys have socks that cover their *calves*, while the girls have socks up to their *knees*. Mother has *stockings* and *pointed* blue shoes. Father has a *moustache* and wears *glasses*. His suit has three *pockets* that can be seen, and others that are covered. Mother's *cheeks* are red, and so are her *lips*. Her eyes are blue as are those of all the children. Father's eyes are greyish-green. He is *going bald*, though his hair is still *dark*.

This study may be pursued even further if more detail is added to the picture.

The technique will be to have the picture on the board while the teacher is introducing each item by saying the word and/or writing it down. After this, questions such as "Is there another hat? Who is wearing it? Who can come and show me all the hats? and tell me who is without a hat?" can be put in the foreign language. The context of the picture serves as an integrative schema. The learning of the words for the objects, introduced with qualifying adjectives, provides the necessary practice and allows the transfer of the responsibility for learning to the students. The teacher could also write on the board around the picture the words as they are met. The students could put them down on their own copy of the picture, and use them orally in class and in writing in their worksheets. They can also be collated in a logbook under a variety of classifications (alphabetically, or by meaning: anatomy, footwear, etc.). Each word does not appear on the board more than once, so as to give rise to exercises in associating names with parts of the drawing. These are left to the class, which accepts or rejects the answer given by any one student. The teacher's job is over when he supplies the first name for the item which he has singled out in the picture.

Drawing No. 9 shows the interior of a shop, a food store with one section selling groceries and dairy products, the other vegetables, fruit and flowers.

The vocabulary is wide and varied. Cans of *soup, meat, coffee, jams, biscuits, cakes, sugar, salt, pepper, spices, powdered milk, cereals, soaps, butter, cheeses, oils* and *fats, bread, soft drinks* in *bottles* or in *cans, vinegar, ham, sausages, matches, fuels, frozen foods; fresh vegetables: salads, cabbage, cauliflower, celery, leeks, mushrooms; seasonal flowers: roses, carnations, violets; fruit: oranges, apples, pears, bananas, grapes,* etc.

Worksheets for use with the drawings

Each student is provided with a worksheet on which he will find reproduced the pictures of the series. Around each, there is space to insert the words studied in the lesson. The worksheets are not to be marked by the teacher (though he will find in them information about the students' progress and effort), but they tell each user how much he has retained of the lessons *at any one moment*. He can always correct himself when he finds that he has made some mistake.

As he works through the questions, he will find that more and more comes back to him and, that at the end perhaps, even most of the vocabulary is well established.

After the page on which the picture is reproduced, there are three pages with either questions or instructions for various exercises:

8) a. Rewrite the following list so as to put together the words concerning dress (d), footwear (f), anatomy (a), ornaments (o), family (F), others (O).

buttonhole	*handbag*	*necklace*	*glass*
shoes	*earring*	*vest*	*wrist*
watch	*ribbon*	*daughters*	*head*
gloves	*trousers*	*bracelet*	*feathers*
hat	*hand*	*belt*	*sons*
stockings	*handkerchief*	*sleeves*	*socks*

b. Make sentences using at least three of the following words in each. Use any others that you wish, including plurals.

head	*father*	*hair*	*gloves*
hat	*waist*	*arm*	*hand*
wrist	*jacket*	*dress*	*ribbon*
girl	*boy*	*mother*	*eyes*
handbag	*socks*	*knees*	*handkerchief*

58

c. Make as many sentences as you can to describe something you can see in the picture or that you believe to be true of the people shown in it.

9) a. Rewrite the following list so as to put together words concerning fruit (f), consumable goods (g) or food to be cooked (c), roots (r).

leek	juices	sugar	syrup
biscuits	apples	sandwiches	celery
oranges	beetroot	greens	potatoes
bread	carrots	roses	pears
cakes	ham	onion	matches

b. Make sentences using at least three of the following words in each. Use any others that you wish, including plurals.

grocer	flowers	oil	bananas
sausages	fruit	vegetables	cabbage
mushroom	spices	meat	ham
roots	cucumber	lettuce	salad
tomato	corn	cereals	oats

c. Make as many sentences as you can to describe something that you can see in the picture, or that you believe to be true of what is shown in it.

2. USE OF TRANSPARENCIES

Whenever teachers have the facilities to show the transparencies prepared for general presentation, the series will serve as an opportunity for widening of experience of the countries whose languages are being studied and for oral work with the whole class. Whereas the drawings were *ad hoc* material for the introduction of sets of words, the transparencies cover selected natural scenes and certain

59

monuments of the countries concerned. As with all our materials, the order given here is simply a suggestion.

The first frame is a map of the country. On a first showing, one could put into circulation the words for *map, country, capital, sea, rivers*, and *mountains.* On a second or third showing, some time later, the same map can serve to introduce *north, east, west, south, boundaries, counties* (or equivalents), *cities, towns, villages, railways, canals, airports, deltas, river mouths, estuaries, islands, harbors, capes, peninsulas, lakes,* etc.

The frames that immediately follow show a countryside scene, a port with its installations, a main street scene in a provincial town, a railway station on a busy day, and a traffic jam with a policeman. These will provide at least some of the following vocabulary:

For the countryside: *fields, meadows, hedges, furrows, crops, tractors, compounds, mills, silos, road, lane, marsh, clouds, horizon, trees, bushes, grass, flowers, blossom, hills, valley, farms, cattle, sheep, pigs,* etc.

For the port: *quay, dock, crane, ship, funnel, mast, boat, bollard, rope, anchor, docker, loading, customs-house, truck, crates, deck, stevedore, sailor, gangway, rudder, portholes,* etc.

For the main street: *shops, shopping center, pavement, town hall, tower, clock, shoppers, busses, cars, news-stand, shoe-shop, bakery, chemist, Post Office, parking lot, restaurant,* etc.

For a railway station: *train, carriage, compartment, luggage, porter, platform, ticket, ticket-office, express, engine, rails, guard, mail, parcels, passengers, waiting-room,* etc.

For the traffic jam: *policeman, traffic lights, motorists, cross-roads, rotary, line, trucks, road, angry, impatient, horn, uniform, helmet,* etc.

The tranparencies show scenes that will give both images from the country and material for new vocabulary:

A well-known monument
An important bridge
A place in the capital
A display of newspapers and magazines
A big airport
An important square in the capital by night
The rush-hour
Children at school
Children at play
A motorway
National costumes or folklore scenes
Musical instruments and music
Inside shops: machinery
                  television and radio
                  a big store
Billboards
Old and new side-by-side
Showrooms: cars
                 electricity board
The interior of a home
People
People
People
A scene in the zoo
A scene in the park
A scene in a market place

Worksheets for use with the transparencies

Since most of the material put into circulation during the showing of the scenes is oral, and the students do not write any of it down, the worksheets that go with the frames will have to rescue most of the vocabulary and propose exercises which will bring the words back into use.

To each frame are devoted four pages of a worksheet.

Page 1 Write down as many as possible of the words you

61

heard when looking at Frame no. ——. If you can, give a drawing of the things described by each of them.

Page 2 With the words above, make as many sentences as you can, including any additional words you wish to use.

The third and fourth pages are devoted to special questions related to the content of the particular frame, thus covering more and more varied ground and vocabulary.

For example, for the motorway, the corresponding pages of the worksheets may be as follows:

Page 3 Look at the sign at the side of the road. What do the various words or symbols on it mean?

Which unit system is used in that country?

On which side of the road does the traffic travel?

What is the speed limit?

What else do you see in this picture that is of interest to you?

Page 4 Write down all the words you know that refer:

to cars

to travel by road

to roads

to the traffic regulations

to the countryside through which a motorway may run

to possible conditions *on* the roads or *of* the roads

To answer some of these questions may require that the frame be projected again and examined carefully.

3.   USE OF FILMS AND TELEVISION PROGRAMS

There are three types of film that can serve our purposes: those made specially for this approach, those made for other approaches, and finally all films made for the public.

The first set will include only background material, associating chatter and images in order to create in the learner a simultaneous experience of sounds and images, and the reality of as many people as possible using the language among themselves.

The second type, being the work of other language teachers, could be used either to supplement this approach or to compare the various approaches and their ways of using the medium of film for linguistic education.

The third type has been produced for quite different purposes than language teaching, but can be considered as an invaluable help to teachers. Documentaries made for general release are often beautiful, and although too expensive to be produced for non-commercial ends, they could be rented by audio-visual departments of schools, for teachers who want to use them. Filmed history, plays or novels are part of the riches of the culture whose language is being studied. They will provide background material that will help the formation of images connected with the people whose spirit is to be felt and experienced with all one's senses, so that the gates of understanding may be opened.

Now that more and more schools use the increasing number of educational television programs, it seems clear that this tool will prove of great assistance for the extension of vocabulary in various directions.

4. TEXTS

Printed texts may be less powerful than films but they are more handy. Material that can be used with little extra equipment can, of course, reach any learner anywhere and satisfy some of his requirements. Here we wish to outline the use of texts prepared for the extension of vocabulary.

Until now, we have used a mixture of oral and written work to ensure that sound always accompanies images or written signs. Now we revert to print as a bridgehead to extend the territory already conquered.

63

a) A collection of sentences which are to be read separately may be one of the ways of providing the bridge. Ideally, each sentence should not contain more than one new word and serves as a support to convey its meaning, such as "This is a house" but in "Our nose is used for smelling and breathing,"

or "The poor little rabbit was caught by the leg in the trap,"

or "That fat man has lost all his money and is now bankrupt,"

it may be impossible to restrict oneself to one new word per sentence.

b) A second collection of sentences is to be read consecutively. In addition to the meaning of each sentence, they will convey an overall meaning which will change the set into a story and will sustain interest of the readers through the desire to know what happens. Moreover, it will provide education of continuous reading habits in the language studied. Here is one of the set of sentences:

The shy man was waiting for the girl behind a tree — she was getting ready to go to her friend's house — it was on the other side of the wood — she did not think anything would happen to her on the way — the man was waiting and thinking: she can't be very long now — a few minutes later the girl appeared at one end of the lane — she could not see the man — he could see her very well and was getting ready to come out and talk to her — she came closer and closer to him — he felt something different every moment, one moment that he would come out and talk to her, and the next that he might frighten her and make her angry with him — when she was almost level with the tree, he made himself long and thin so that she did not see him and passed by — he held his breath for a minute till she was out of sight at the other end of the lane — he sat down at the foot of the tree not knowing what he was doing or why.

c) A third text is a book of stories of some length, through which the vocabulary will branch out into the normal use of language so as to consider almost everything through words alone.

The eight tales in this book have been told in a number of languages in a number of lands and to listeners from seven to seventy years old. Because they appeal to such a wide audience, they have been included in this program, which is not confined to any age groups.

Worksheets

The last set of worksheets is about the language as a whole, with no restriction upon vocabulary or composition. It follows the same expansion as the three texts.

a) First, we make sentences and look at them. This provides an opportunity to consider structure and meet grammatical functions. The set of word-cards can be used for this purpose, as they display in the color of the card an index that enables the learners to discover that words printed on cards of the same color have something in common: grammatical function.

In the beginning of the work, the learners look at one sentence printed on the worksheet, and go to the word-cards to make the sentence with them. This will give them some indication that such and such a word somehow belongs to such and such another, which may not be as easily perceived in the printed sentence alone.

The first question is: which of the words in this sentence can be removed without altering the main meaning? which cannot?

For instance, "I have a very lovely daughter whom I love very dearly" can become "I have a daughter whom I love," and can provide a succession of sentences between these.

The second question is: make sentences which have exactly the same pattern as the one above, but use very different words and convey a different thought. (In lessons at school, we would have already been doing such exercises orally and with the whole class.) For example: "Mr. Smith has a very heavy suitcase which he carries very slowly."

The third question is: if you can, make the following sentence longer without altering its meaning. For example: "I am cold" may step by step become

"Winter is here, and whenever I stop walking I am cold." *or* "There is frost around, the trees are bare, and when I cross the field I am cold and lonely." *or* "I am cold because I got up early, had no breakfast and had to wait in the street for the office to open."

The fourth question is: make as many sentences as you can out of the words of the following sentence. "As they were good friends, he and she did not often quarrel" can give among others the following:

he and she quarrel often
did they often quarrel?
he and she were good friends
théy were often good.

b) Secondly, we look at a group of sentences to see what links we can find between some of them to change a set into a story or stories.

For example, from the five sentence: the cup was empty — a shot was heard at a reception in the big hotel — a woman suddenly ran away — the silence became heavy — everything is very sad, we can form:

A shot was heard at a reception in the big hotel, a woman suddenly ran away, the silence became heavy, everything is very sad.

The cup was empty, a shot was heard, the silence became heavy.

A similar exercise is to add words to the sentences of each group to make them part of a story.

With the above, for example, we can form the following text if we add the underlined words:

66

As the shot was heard at a reception in the big hotel, a woman suddenly ran away; the cup was empty *and* the silence became heavy.

When the shot was heard the cup was empty, . . .

Teachers will think out variations of more interest to them, and so be more successful with their own classes.

c) Thirdly, we consider the Book of Stories and see that, although it is a series of acceptable texts taking us presumably where the author wants, the words he uses may not always be the only ones that would serve the purpose, nor is the end of each story one that could not be altered by adding paragraphs of one's own.

This series of exercises is meant to start the students working on a text in order to analyze it for the language it contains or for what could be generated from it by analogy, alterations, and so on. It is also designed to give the students an opportunity for literary study.

The purpose of an author in producing a story is to interest his readers and himself, and to create a climate in which he may surreptitiously convey what matters to him at the time of writing. So we can look at a text to find the various layers of the integrative schemata. First, we clearly see that each sentence "belongs" to the story because events it relates are linked to others by direct reference, by the assumed permanence of the characters introduced, or by other assumptions which we may make since writers take advantage of them all the time: the scene remains the same as long as it is not stated categorically that it has changed; the ages of the people do not alter at random; the reference to a period is maintained, etc. Secondly, we may know that the motif of the story is dictated by the writer's desire to bring readers to feel with him on matters that are important for him: love for animals, a socialist solution of economic problems, temperance or vegetarianism, etc. This deeper intention holds the story before the story holds the events, the events the statements and the statements phrases and words. Literary insights may stop at different levels of penetration of the integrative schemata. Discussion of sample texts at school and questions in the worksheets may draw attention to their existence, why they matter, and how they operate. A consequence will be "better" reading.

Besides these two aspects of the study of a work of art made of printed words, there remain the important questions of effectiveness of style, of selected vocabularies, and their impact, of the varieties of expression in one and the same work, and what purpose they may serve.

Naturally, no one would expect exhaustive study of any one of these insights by any one of the learners. Nevertheless, they will be mentioned for those who are attracted in such a direction. Moreover, if teachers realize that whenever they do something with a given text, they are at the same time leaving out something else, they will develop a relationship with the texts which I believe will eventually become an alertness towards opportunities from which students may benefit greatly.

The third part of the worksheets is therefore devoted to literary awareness in the foreign language, though for young students who have little time to give to this, simple realistic questions are included. Teachers will find that they can expand these sections indefinitely.

5. ANTHOLOGIES

Our pupils will have had opportunities to work on language as a vehicle for communication concerning many topics, useful and perhaps even important for everyday living. They will have reached a level of familiarity with the idiosyncrasies of the language which eliminates these as obstacles for progress. They may even enjoy looking at things in another way than that of their neighbors who do not possess such insights. Language has been studied for itself, both in relation to statements of fact and concerning a kind of abstract knowledge related to structure, to what is permissible and what would sound incorrect. With the Book of Stories we started considering another dimension of the written language — style. It can now be found that natives often use their written and spoken languages in different ways, that the majority write as they speak, but some speak as if they were writing, while the rest have one style for literary writing and one for daily use including conversation. Some languages are dominated by the spoken and others by the written, language.

There is clearly a fascinating field of enquiry here from which education could draw some advantages.

For our purpose, it is enough to start our learners off. We propose to do so first by focussing on styles of writing, then on writing and individuality, and finally on style and art.

Our *First Anthology* is made of a succession of short texts (about 500 words) taken from authors who have passed hurdles and have become literary figures of their time. At the first glance one can say that there are writers who use short sentences and others who use longer ones, but that simple statement is replaced by a much more shaded one when we look more closely into the writing of a number of authors whose texts are included in the anthology. Reading these authors one after the other will show that sentence-making is fashioned by what one wishes to convey, and how the dialogue between the author and the reader is established. Does one want to win agreement gradually or does one want to shock and to jolt? Can one jolt with long sentences? Can one win agreement by making short statements? Can one give descriptions equally well using either long or short sentences, or does one need a blend of the two to do it adequately? To maintain the reader's interest, does it matter whether one writes long or short sentences? What sort of interest does one wish to arouse? Can one be subjective and write short sentences, or is it necessary to use winding ones full of incidental clauses? Conversely, can one be objective with a similar style? Is style a function of the structure of the language? (Students who only know two languages may not be able to decide on this matter through direct experience for a long time.) Can one find examples of all styles in all languages? If the answer is in the affirmative, then the previous question is also answered: if it is in the negative, it is not necessarily an answer to the previous question — investigation is still required.

The first anthology (one for each language for which we have published materials) is therefore a succession of texts to display styles.

Our *Second Anthology* is also made of short passages (about 500 words), but this time there are a certain number by the same author, so as to examine whether "style is the man" (Buffon), or whether authors, like actors who play differently when acting vastly different parts, have as many styles as they have fields of writing.

If style is the man, reading is a way into other sensitivities, as well as into other experiences.

If style is an artifact, we will have to study deeper dimensions of the writing, and also sociological, historical and biographical material to reach the author as a person.

This anthology is not produced with a ready-made answer to that question. It sets out to make a dual contribution: on the one hand, we want to place the student squarely in front of a question which is both linguistic and human, and on the other hand, we want to contribute to literary awareness as we hope to have contributed to linguistic awareness. Much of what the learners have been doing for months is concerned with language as the vehicle, and has only partly served as a bridge between immediacy and other uses of the language. We now provide an opportunity for the student to see the deferred language (of necessity written or nowadays recorded) at work. Writers reach the impossible: they objectify the fleeting moment that runs away with speech. But, more than that, they keep alive among us the kind of human experience that goes into the making of traditions. So the written language, though connected in so many ways with the spoken, differs from it in its degree of objectivity, in its graspability, in its capacity for impact, etc. To study the written language is to add to one's insight as much as to one's vocabulary, but it is mainly to shift the emphasis from language as a tool to language as one of man's modes of expression. The study of the great writers is hence the school for lifting oneself from the level of communication with others to the level of communication with the seers and through them to what life has to offer us in terms of events, attitudes, growth of sensitivity and experiences, insights into what matters or mattered or may matter most.

Our *Third Anthology* is our present answer for the introduction to a promised land.

Every editor of an anthology has a criterion. Mine is that I wish to give my approach the support I can find in the works of great writers. My aim is the education of spiritual powers and sensitivity in the individual. The learners, many of whom will be adolescents, will spontaneously be in contact with their own expanding self, knowing intimately what power is in its somatic, psychic and intellectual guises. The texts I present here are about four times longer than those used in the two previous anthologies. They may be a full short story or a scene of a play or a chapter in a novel or a letter, a pamphlet, a poem or a section of a chapter. They have been chosen because they show that in the foreign language all or most literary

71

forms have been cultivated; because the authors who are represented have made an impact on the people whose language is being studied; because the passages selected add something vital to everyone, whether he is a member of the author's group or a "foreigner," and because of the literary values of the text. Thus a detailed study of all these texts will be both educational in the wider sense and informative in the strictly cultural sense. Although the students of these texts may be spending all their language periods on one language, for a number of years, we should not exclude the thought that some contact with the third anthology could be a possibility even for first-year learners of any age. Time is of the essence, as well as interest and maturity, but these are not identical with age.

It is easy enough to select texts to form an anthology and, with luck, to produce a collection that people will enjoy reading. But, as literary material, the texts must be studied and progress reported. Teachers will wish to have some indication of how their students are to use these texts.

Three uses can be foreseen for this anthology, in addition to its function as an inducement to read the whole works from which the extracts have been taken. (At the moment, worksheets are not intended for the anthologies.)

1. A series of questions can be asked about each text.

Collect words and expressions new to you, and find out what they are about. Are they worth retaining? Explain why.

What sort of speech is being used (personal, direct, figurative)?

Write a précis of this text in, say, 100 words.

Characterize this writer's style.

Write a short biography of the author.

Can you see one or more possible continuations of the passage you read? Which one did the author choose? If you read the whole book, you will be able to answer this question, as well as "Why?"

Some of these questions are obvious, and already appear, amongst others, in a number of the texts used for language teaching. New ones could be asked, drawing attention to peculiarities either in the text, or about the author's special use of literary devices. For example: is there a particular way of starting a chapter or a paragraph? Can one see the difference between the tone of a sentence in its beginning and its end? Does this author obey rules for paragraphing, punctuation, etc.? What do you feel about this text that you have never experienced with another one?

2. Because these texts are longer than those in the first two anthologies, we can ask questions arising from the reader's longer exposure to each author through his writing.

Is this text an exposition, a narrative, an argument, etc.?

Has the writer impressed you by his style? his sense of humor? the content of the text, or the examples given?

Can you say what are the salient qualities of this piece of writing?

Do you find yourself in sympathy with the argument (if there is one) or with the material presented?

Can you improve upon what use is made of the evidence?

Would you look at things as the author does?

Has the experience of reading this text done something to you? What?

Should this text be more widely read? Why?

3. The third use is much more elaborate and creative, and could serve in literature to give more advanced learners experience of styles, just as musicians can compose *à la manière de* Ravel, Dubussy, or Mozart and still have their own style.

To practice such "games", one can use a number of periods in which people listen, with their eyes shut, to a good reader reading a passage of any one of the texts, and have to guess who has written it. If this exercise is correctly carried out, it tells us that the listeners now have an ear for styles. It is possible that some of the students may guess almost at the first sentence, if the author's style is so characteristic, or if they have really developed such sensitivity to style, or else if their memory is such that they know who wrote which extract in that book, in which case another anthology should, of course, be used.

After a successful trial of this kind, themes could be proposed for attempts to write *à la manière de* x, y or z.

If these exercises are also successful, each learner will have at his disposal an arsenal of styles in contrast to or according to which he may form his own.

Naturally, much of what has been said about the third anthology and its uses can be done more easily with the mother tongue, but I personally have used it for foreign languages. The adoption of such approaches in the study of foreign literatures may require us first to make sure that our students are sufficiently mature, and can handle the language competently. There are two possibilities to keep in mind. One is that there may be highly gifted students who may want to be challenged by such meaningful games which require sophistication in the approach to the written word. Through these exercises they will also improve their grasp of structure. But we must not forget those who can only attempt a hurdle when they feel secure enough. For them, we should postpone the presentation of any such games till they ask for them. There is little doubt that some will.

Most languages which people wish to learn are already endowed with original literatures, and we will have little trouble in getting a list of the best volumes available.

In most countries there are cheap editions that could provide a good library at a minimal expenditure.

We do not advocate that each country publish annotated texts for their foreign language students, except as a transitional measure. For if this approach is truly carried out as we recommend, the level of understanding of a foreign language will reach that of the mother tongue.

We often find very good translations of the masterpieces of world literature. There is no doubt that the reading of such translations as books in one's own language, and not related to the demands of the study of the foreign language, will serve us better if they are not disrupted by references to notes and glossaries. The integrative schema of the story carried in one's mind and independent of language (though not of culture) will play a unifying role and will sustain the efforts one has to make when coping with the book in the original.

5.   What Results Can We Expect?

I hope that in the previous chapters I have been able to impress upon teachers that I am a teacher myself, preoccupied with classroom work and concerned with activities which generate successful language learning.

As this chapter follows my practical suggestions, it will be easier to assess what can be expected from working in the way I have proposed, referring where necessary to specific exercises.

For the first group of lessons with beginners, lasting perhaps a term, it is clear that the use of the rods and the first few wallcharts will suffice to convey what was discussed in Chapter 3. In some cases, for these sixty or so lessons eight charts may be too many.

As we saw in Chapter 3, the printed word is introduced quite early. Since by the age of seven the students will have written down some kind of statement in their mother tongue, it will be possible to add oral dictation to Visual Dictation.

The techniques themselves and the design of the materials provide a permanent system for checking the learner's progress. There is no need for correction by the teacher. Since the teacher's role here is not to purvey knowledge, he can stand back and watch the students correcting themselves and making alternative suggestions to what is offered by their classmates. Marking can be reduced to gathering scores kept by the students themselves, plus an overall mark for the work done during a certain period of days or weeks. As tests are an integral part of the approach, there will be no difficulty in knowing objectively how far the students have moved.

The worksheets are self-scoring and each student works on them at different stages of his progress. He can take up different challenges at different levels of his proficiency, and can measure what he knew earlier against what he knows now.

After the first few weeks, we begin with the material described in Chapter 4. There again, because of the way we develop the powers of the learners, there will be no need for the teacher to do more than to watch, challenge, encourage and study the products of the individual and collective efforts of the learners.

We have made sure from the outset that students listen to their own voices and watch all their utterances, both with respect to pronunciation and with respect to content. If this is properly carried out the immediate formation of the inner criteria will be obvious. Firstly, the students will have a really good diction in the new language, with a clear pronunciation of each word (as close as possible to that of natives) and an easy flow in sentence-making, observing the melodic line of that language. Secondly, the students will feel and think in the new language, as will be evident from the correctness of their speech.

They will easily accept that their teacher never uses the vernacular and is inaccessible through it.

Because the teacher has never demanded immediate perfection, the relationship between him and his class will be conducive to constant re-examination of what can be done and what is being done. Improvement is visible suddenly and all the time: all the time through the awareness of what one is doing, and suddenly when a deeper understanding of the possibilities or of the requirements has taken place.

Teachers who refrain from pushing students who do not seem to respond or attempt to participate will be rewarded one day when these students join in as if they had never been out. Indeed, we cannot point to the particular needs of each mind to overcome the real or imaginary obstacles it is meeting. We can help more frequently and more effectively if we stop interfering.

It has been my repeated experience that whenever I am in doubt about a student's reasons for not joining in and I suspend action on, or reaction to him, the outcome is success at a later date. But whenever I enter too forcefully or too quickly into a situation of which I have inadequate understanding, my students entrench themselves in an uncooperative mood that does not serve anyone.

The pattern of progress in the gaining of skills is now well known. At first there is random or almost random feeling of the area of activity in question until one finds one or more cornerstones to build on. Then starts a systematic analysis, first by trial and error, later by directed experiment with practice of the acquired subareas until mastery follows. Emotionally, this mastery brings an inner peace which shows that one is not anxious about the results any longer. Intellectually, it shows that another level of awareness has been reached from which one can survey all activities of the past related to this area of experience. It is then that one suddenly appears to be a different person, both to oneself and to the observers. The learner's actions in this new area of experience reveal maturity and self-confidence. This provides constant confirmation of his control over his learning and gives a sense of power which is accompanied by efficiency.

Because the learner is now in control and operates with increased power, he can tackle larger tasks and more challenging developments. He can repeat the cycle of contact, analysis, mastery, not only for a different content, but also at a different tempo. This I call the cumulative effect of learning, and it is one of the results I expect through the silent approach.

If, therefore, after one term we have mastered the large integrative schemata that will facilitate the conquest of vocabularies, we can expect that little memorization will be required, while much retention of related words will be experienced. Indeed, memory is a function of concentration in most of us (I exclude the pathological cases mentioned in the literature on memory). We can see this at work in very young children, who are more concentrated than the older ones and retain much more and much faster than the older ones do. We can expect that less and less repetition will be needed to reach greater retention of vocabulary and enrichment of one's analytic knowledge of a language for more specialized uses. Perhaps if the technique mentioned in various places — that the learner alone is to decide when repetition is needed — is tried out, it will be found that its yield in remembered expressions is incomparably greater than that of repetition. In fact, repetition consumes time and encourages the scattered mind to remain scattered, whereas the teacher's strict avoidance of repetition forces alertness and concentration on the part of the learners. In my experience, this increases yield and efficiency, and saves time for further learning.

All this tells us that it is no longer utopian to conceive that in *one* school year we will be able not only to reach

80

but, I believe, to surpass what is otherwise achieved in four. It is for this reason that in the description of the materials and the lessons I have not suggested any fixed time as required for the conquest of vocabulary, nor have I suggested any one stage of achievement as final. If after experimentation with this approach, people agree with me, then they can safely take up another language in the following year and expect that, precisely because of the cumulative effect of learning, it will be more easily mastered than the previous one. But, as I said earlier, this is not the only way open, for any one life is never sufficient to reach a final point in any serious study, and a language is a field that engages scores of investigators. If students wish to continue studying the language after one year, there is plenty of material for the rest of their school career at least. It is for these students that we have included the last section of Chapter 4.

For those who measure achievement through examinations, I will now estimate what can be expected after one year of study of a language through this approach.

In an oral examination, most direct questions about oneself, one's education, one's family, travel, etc., should obtain answers that are correct, expressed with ease and a good accent. Any mistakes will be simply minor slips or else due to a misunderstanding of what was communicated.

If a picture is provided, whether in a written or an oral examination, the student will be able to describe in the foreign language most of what he sees, including the existing relationships that concern space, time and numbers. As writing has been catered for with the charts, with the color-code and various texts, spelling should be more than reasonably good, and, in the case of non-phonetic languages, it should show a definite insight into why alternatives are reduced. As structure has been practiced in a variety of ways (through the ear, Visual Dictation, use of word-cards, reading, writing and talking), grammar should be adequate, which will be implicit in the correct usage, even if all the candidates are not able to formulate it explicitly. Idiosyncrasies of each language have been met as natural features and accepted as given, without comparison and memorization. So candidates would know what to do even if they did not yet know why.

Translations are possible, for in this approach, rather than understanding the text through words checked against words, the learners have passed from text to reality (sensed or imagined). As they can talk directly of such reality (if it is suitably selected) either in their mother tongue or in the other language, translations are direct expressions in either language of what was communicated by the original text. Naturally, we expect that the essence of a situation, as expressed by the functional vocabulary which is present in a given text, will not be missed, and that only the luxury components could be overlooked or wrongly grasped, hence mistranslated. Translation is an art for the specialist, not for the novice.

We can expect questions on a selected text to be handled adequately, as on the whole (provided they are not too sophisticated) they come naturally to the mind of a reader who has been asked from the start, and all the time, to consider texts as linguistic situations.

General questions about the culture of the peoples who use the languages studied should be satisfactorily answered. As we have taken care of extending the vocabulary with texts belonging to that culture, through documentary films that are full of information for the learner, and as we have considerably assisted the learners in reaching the spirit of the language through its sociological and historical components, it is clear that students who have learned in that way will be incomparably better equipped than students taken through traditional approaches or direct methods that are purely linguistic. The benefits gained from the alertness fostered by this approach can be seen again in the amount of incidental learning that takes place, with the materials designed to give cultural awareness implicitly even if no lessons are devoted to it; and also explicitly if one cares to do so and can find the time for it.

The interest in reading, and the availability of the whole of literature in the language studied may extend to all students a situation known to exist in the case of some: they like to read the original works and do read a great deal for their own enjoyment and cultivation. If literary questions are to be included in a certain examination, they should be answered satisfactorily by these students. The novelty will be that many more candidates may be interested in answering them and will be able to do so quite well.

To sum up what I believe to be reasonable to expect from an approach like this — and I am willing to be assessed on the results of colleagues giving it a fair trial — I would list the following:

• An accent as close as possible to that of the natives who are among really cultured members of the country whose language is being studied.

• From the start, an ease in conversation related to the vocabularies presented and studied.

• An ease at dictation with speeds related to the amount of Visual Dictation practiced and the difficulties of the text.

• An ease in composition about all topics whose vocabularies have been met.

• An ease at narrating events, describing pictures, at shopping in various shops, ordering in hotels and restaurants, and at asking for directions, etc.

• An ability to render appropriate texts of either language into the other.

Additional questions will require first that one should know whether the learners have actually passed the level of study of the language as a vehicle and reached the level where the literature can be studied as a depository of the language and of its spirit.

A word in conclusion. In this book, written for a public wider than that of foreign language specialists, I have attempted to add new challenges to what learners and their teachers usually meet; but I believe I have also added many more helpful techniques and materials.

Often we hear that language studies are essential today because of the shrinking world and for the sake of international understanding. I have considered that question elsewhere, at the time when I directed the International Training Institute and ran international seminars for human education, in which people of various countries and languages participated. Linguistic studies, like all others, may be a specialization, and they carry with them a narrow opening of one's sensitivity and perhaps serve very little towards the broad end in mind.

If we now develop language teaching in such a way as to consolidate the human dimensions of being, which include variety and individuality as essential factors for an acceptance of others as contributors to one's own life, I believe that we will be moving towards better and more lasting solutions of present-day conflicts. These, to my mind, are the outcome of our living on top of each other, our sensitivities turned inward, restricting ourselves, when we need to be absorbing others as they *are* in an enhanced and more open sensitivity.

To that end this silent way of teaching is devoted.

Figure I

une réglette -s moi a

jaune j'ai bleue noire

verte avons ici brune

aussi elle rouge vous

donnez deux la prenez

avez ils elles ont à

lui il et les oui nous

notre leur mettez sa

là ma votre est non

French
Wallchart number 1

a rod -s -s blue

green yellow black

brown take red give

as to it and not

back here her is the

them two him an me

orange the are one he

another these white

put end too his

English as a second languge
Wallchart number 1

Appendix:
The Silent Way
in The Classroom

The various sections of this part of the book have been contributed in complete freedom by each of the writers. At a planning session it was only agreed that we must avoid being repetitive, and that together these contributions would cover a sufficiently large area to serve teachers of beginners, of intermediate and of advanced students of any age.

The contributors were quick at fulfilling their promise. They showed me that they are not only the users of an approach but also true supporters of a sensible way of teaching foreign languages. To each will go my warmest thanks as well as the appreciation of the readers who will recognize that without this last section the book would be much poorer.

While learning to teach by the Silent Way, each of the writers has had plenty of opportunities to observe the classes of students studying the language he or she offers.

What we find in their writings is a constellation of diverse approaches to the Silent Way, all of which evoke real people who attended the classes. Had there been more reports, more diversity would have been the outcome.

This tells me that the Silent Way is one way of humanizing the teaching of foreign languages in schools, and of taking care of the human components in the classrooms of the world. Still, because it is teachers who are writing, the message is one concerned with language teaching and some of the hardest problems that a particular language presents. These considerations are valuable because the readers can realize that the writers are not only the enthusiasts who are speaking about what they like but also the technicians who are solving difficult problems met by all teachers. Perhaps there are not enough technical hints for those who expect them. The whole book remains only an introduction, and more detailed literature will develop as the years go by.

For the moment, the creative teachers are producing the tools for their trade, which seem to be the charts, not yet composed, and ways of using them which permit safe progress of the students. However clear the content of these charts, related to situations which are generated with the colored rods, only intimacy with them, in class after class after class, will create the real peace of mind that frees the users. The only errors visible to observers who are watching lessons given by the Silent Way teachers are those concerned with the position of the teacher between the student and the charts, the way the pointer is held, and the rhythm of pointing at various stages in their use. But the invisible errors can only be perceived by the teacher who is doing the teaching. The silence allows one to concentrate on the feedback from the students and to notice whether none, one or many are left out of the lesson. Teachers may not see at once that their students' responses are all they have to go by in shaping each move in their lesson. Only then will it be possible to notice whether one is involved in teaching the language rather than the students. Indeed, this is both the easiest mistake for teachers of language to make and the hardest one to correct. When the conversion to true teaching takes place, all errors seem to be corrected at once. After that one welcomes slips or daring moves which can generate traps from which one can learn better how to make one's Silent Way more precise.

The Silent Way is but a way. It is not a structural or a linguistic or a direct (or any other) method of teaching languages. In the hands of expert teachers the materials would lose their predominance, the teacher his dominant role, the language its appearance as *the* target. Instead, everything and everybody serves one aim, to make everyone into the most competent learner. This is the function of learning. Learning is not seen as the means of accumulating knowledge but as the means of becoming a more proficient learner of whatever one is engaged in. The appearance itself supports this conclusion: one learns more and faster in equal durations as time goes by.

The outsiders who are only the onlookers may even say that this is a powerful way of teaching, but they will not know why. What is invisible, but is there, is the fact that the "linguistic muscle" is becoming stronger through exercises. This permits the attack of larger tasks which serve as further exercises that will extend one's capacity to attack still larger tasks. Besides a muscle, a sensitivity that has also been developed allows the learners to discriminate among the practices which foster the development of the muscle and those that hinder it. Students can now select to do exercises that serve them rather than waste their time. The appetite for larger "meals" grows, and lessons cover much more ground as time goes on.

At the beginning we move slowly while meeting

what is qualified as the hardest part of the new language, the peculiarities which may not exist in the native tongue of the learners. This daring is justified by the common knowledge that one does not use a language in successive approximations, always improving one's uses. On the contrary, once they get into the faulty uses, most people never get out of them. The learning of a language outside early childhood is one in which one uses all one has to concentrate on acquiring what one does not yet have. By restricting the extent of the language to be presented and to be worked on, the teacher provides the greatest chances of using perception, intelligence and any valid clues to reach a level of functioning in the new language comparable to the one used in one's own language.

But to generate the restricted languages which greatly facilitate learning, we must provide freedom for the students to express what seems right to them in a given context. This can only be obtained through proper *transformations*, not through the repetition of what is heard. Hence, generally speaking, functional words are given in clusters with clues that produce the transformations which lead to correct usage.

From this alone we have learned that each lesson is a beautiful challenge to our imagination. We must find out what to do and how much to say so that our students get such a feel of the new language that they spontaneously *invent* correct forms with as much assurance as they did in their first year of life. A field of research opens up here: which forms in each particular language could be invented? by whom? and how? to be followed by another research: can this teach us something about the original generation of the languages of the world?

Each mistake made by students or teachers can be of help in the study of the linguistic functioning of man. We need to know this functioning in the making, and no better place exists for that than among the serious learners engaged in the dual learning of a language and of the learning process.

Many curtains will be lifted when we are sufficiently numerous and sufficiently serious to allow all the flowing evidence to guide our conscious study. We will, for instance, dare ask questions that only crazy people would formulate, such as: "How did language come about?", "What had people done to themselves to reach the awareness that sounds could serve as signals for intellectual expression?", etc. These questions take us back to the remotest times in the prehistory of mankind and into very early childhood.

Teachers have so often held that their job is to correct mistakes, that they neither noticed that only each learner can correct himself, nor have they studied how people finally arrive at the correct use of a language, and what role mistakes play in the learning process.

In particular, most teachers (and for that matter not only language teachers) failed to recognize the role of sleep in the learning process. Sleep is the return to one's integrity and one's freedom, to the continuity of our personal life interrupted by the random or routine events of one's social life. We sleep to restore ourselves; but not only physically, psychically and mentally, too. Hence all learning which involves the somatic, psychic and spiritual parts of man will go on during the phase of sleep when we sift and reconsider what is left in us by the impacts of the day.

In the study of languages much of what is decisive takes place during the night's sleep. Users of the Silent Way know how to wait for the return of their class after a night's sleep in order to consider whether the exercises of the previous day have been effective. Often they report that what seemed chaotic the day before was smooth and acceptable the next day.

To correct ourselves we need criteria and these are perhaps at work during the sleeping state as much as during the waking state, some more effectively in one than in the other. In the case of skills, our finding is that sleep serves us better in our improvements than our awake reflection. This important additional contribution of the Silent Way to the study of learning in general may find its way in all classrooms where students will be trusted more because they are responsible learners in school and outside of it.

What all the contributors here are saying is that to subordinate teaching to learning works in the field of languages. Together we say: this is not a method or a device or a system or a program, but it is being sensible and sensitive to the reality of different learning situations. I believe that our work is a contribution to a general study of how people learn, to the science of epistemology that is a necessary basis for sound teaching.

Contributors

Sue Wong was a junior high school social studies teacher in New York City. She gave a number of the Chinese language (Mandarin and Cantonese) courses at Educational Solutions, Inc. Last summer, while on a study trip in Thailand, she lost her life in an accident. A great teacher of language and a clear exponent of the Silent Way disappeared with her.

Jane Orton is an Austrialian who taught French by the Silent Way for three years and conducted seminars on this approach to language teaching in New York City and New Haven. At present, she is teaching English as a second language by the Silent Way in Paris.

Ghislaine Graf, a French speaking Swiss, has been teaching French by the Silent Way to junior high school students, in a school in New York City, and to adults at our intensive weekend and week long courses.

Lolita Goldstein is an experienced teacher of languages to high school students in a private school in Riverdale, N.Y. She has found in the Silent Way a renewal of her enthusiasm as well as sound techniques.

Hilde Jaeckel teaches German and French at Staten Island Community College. Her experiment in teaching by the Silent Way was carried out concurrently with her teaching of French by other approaches.

Cecilia Bartoli Perrault teaches Italian language and literature at New York University. As a student of the Silent Way, she has been instrumental in converting teachers to this approach — particularly at the college level — while preparing her own materials for her classes in the Silent Way.

James Karambelas teaches Russian at the Pingry School in New Jersey. At present on leave of absence in Moscow, he is preparing materials for the teaching of Russian by the Silent Way, while writing his doctoral dissertation.

Maria del Carmen Gagliardo learned the Silent Way as a trainee at Educational Solutions, in New York City, and as an assistant to Dr. Caleb Gattegno. An Argentinian, now residing in New York City, she teaches Spanish at Richmond College, Staten Island.

Rosalyn Bennett is a bilingual teacher (Spanish and English) who adopted the Silent Way in preference to all the approaches she met as an M.A.T. student. Now a consultant in bilingualism and a teacher of adults, she has a wide register of useful experience in the Silent Way.

Robert L. Coe teaches French and Spanish, as well as chairs the Language Department of the Pingry School in Elizabeth, New Jersey.

CHINESE

I had a number of objectives in my teaching of Chinese:

1. To introduce Chinese as a polysyllabic language
2. To introduce tone as an intrinsic characteristic of Chinese, without which the language cannot function
3. To introduce character recognition of the spoken word
4. To introduce basic principles of character writing

A three day workshop, a total of twenty-one hours, taught by the Silent Way, made the students capable of understanding and actively using the basic structures of Chinese in a way that was faithful to the "spirit" of the Chinese language.

Only rods were used to introduce new concepts. This was achieved through introduction of unambiguous linguistic situations which engaged students' perception and invited intellectual guess through which the meaning was reached. The color-keyed charts were used for pronunciation and character recognition. No English was permitted and concepts were introduced only once by me.

The following is a sample of a three day seminar, one of a number of possible ways of creating activities which can generate language learning.

The First Day — I began by picking up several wooden rods and indicating that each was a "mu-tiao" or "a rod." I elicited a response from each student as I picked up the rods one at a time. I then introduced colors: red, green, blue, pink, orange, yellow, white, black, brown, and elicited a response from each student by picking up differently colored rods. I then added the numerals from one to ten and elicited responses like "i-tiao lan mu-tiao" or "one blue rod," etc. After that I introduced "this" and "that" and the verb "to be." We then went into negative sentences and interrogative sentences. At about this point I introduced the vowel sounds on the phonic code chart and also the tones which I demonstrated once and indicated by gestures thereafter. I also introduced, at the end of the day, the verb "to take" and "to give" and the personal pronouns in the nominative, accusative and possessive cases.

The Second Day — I introduced adverbs and positional verb "tsai" to indicate location, "in front of," "behind," "inside," "outside," "on top of," and "at the bottom of." I did so by using a box and the rods in different positions in relation to the box. We also played a game in which I asked the students to pick up different rods and put them in a certain position in relation to one another. Each student did this for the group. I also introduced telling of the time, and the verb "to come" and "to go." I interspersed this with introducing consonants and consonant vowels, first in the color coded chart and then on the character chart. I frequently went back to the chart when the pronunciation was inaccurate to the point where the word being said was distorted. I ended the session by introducing the adjectives "small," "big," "near," "far," "tall," "short" and the idea of comparison of size and distance. Here, again, I used the rods lined up against each other to introduce comparative size. We built "houses" of bricks with roads running between them. We also constructed a school and began comparing distances between different points.

The Third Day — I introduced vocabulary concerned with the members of the family — "mother," "father," "younger brother," "younger sister," "aunt," "uncle," "child," "wife," "husband," "grandmother," "grandfather."

We used the rods to represent members of our own families and had many things to say about them. I also introduced the verb "to have" and the word "tso," meaning "travel," and words like "airplane," "car," "bus," and "ship." I finally introduced the concept "le" to form the past tense. We also attempted to set up situations with the rods and to describe each in Chinese. At the end of the last day, we finished the color-coded chart and the character charts. I had also introduced basic principles of writing of the Chinese characters.

At the end of our third day conversation in Chinese was spirited. Jokes were attempted, as were double entendres. There were stretches of conversation in which I did not participate as a teacher at all.

With regard to the progress made by the students, I want to emphasize strongly the control the teacher must maintain in introducing new concepts. New vocabulary must be introduced through unambiguous situations and already mastered structures should be used to generate new ones. New concepts must be introduced in a logical sequence. For example, for comparative and superlative forms I did the following: I introduced the concept of "large" and "small" with the separate rods. I then set up two rods next to one another and used the comparative form. Afterward, I set up a third rod to demonstrate the superlative. I moved on to a more abstract situation by introducing the concept of distance between two points, and then comparative distances.

This way of working makes it possible for the students

to recognize rhythm, melody, and intonation from the beginning. My students were able to do so, and this recognition of the nonverbal aspects of language enabled them to use naturally structures that have no equivalents in English. An example of this is the use of what is commonly called "classifiers." These are words placed between the number and the noun to indicate a class of nouns. For example: "mu-tiao" would use the classifier "tiao" to indicate a long object; thus, "i-tiao mu-tiao" is "one rod." The number and classifier are pronounced as one phrase. The students in my class were easily able to use the classifier and connect it to the number as one phrase.

This idea of phrasing is directly related to another aspect of Chinese. Most non-Chinese assume Chinese to be monosyllabic. Actually most words are polysyllabic. Again, most of my students were able to understand this concept. For example, "i-tien chung" ("one o'clock") or "mu-tiao ("rod") were all pronounced properly as phrases. This was supported by the use of the character chart as well. I would indicate the phrasing by the proper beat and the combinations of characters which formed the particular phrases were recognized on the chart.

If a teacher understands and employs the basic principles of the Silent Way, and is willing to overcome her old habits and preconceptions about language acquisition, she may expect some of the following results from her class:

1. The disappearance of self-consciousness on the part of the student,

2. Pride in progress the student has made through trial and error,

3. Disappearance of bad habits acquired in previous exposure to a new language,

4. Motivation to continue in the language,

5. Interaction among the class members rather than between the class and the teacher,

6. Rapid progress in the ability of the student to use the foreign language.

Above all, in the Silent Way lessons the learning of a language becomes an enjoyable experience for the teacher and the student, which is an essential element of the learning process itself.

Sue Wong

FRENCH

One of the most powerful advantages of the Silent Way is that it enters the language to be studied at its base: those words, expressions, word orders and so on, which do not necessarily correspond to one's own language, but without which one is totally inarticulate. The concept of "much language and little vocabulary" has seemed to me to be a most valuable one from the time I first heard of the Silent Way in Australia in 1967. At that time a senior at the university, I was overburdened with French and German nouns and pitifully aware of my inability to do much with them.

Those of us who have learned languages, or anything else, through traditional techniques have become used to the idea that what is required of one is to say back to the teacher what has just been said to the class. This includes the echo system (A: Bonjour, comment allez-vous? B. Bonjour, comment allez-vous? A: Bonjour, comment allez-vous? B: Bonjour . . .) and the answering in full sentences system (Est-ce que Marie aime danser? Oui, Marie aime danser).

It takes some time even these days with, say, a group of fifth graders who are meeting their first foreign language, to show them that they will be able to use it in the normal way in which they use their own; so that "Est-ce que vous aimez le cinéma?" may be answered, "Non, pas tellement, je préfère le théâtre." It is in its insistence on throwing the students back onto their inner understanding of what language is and on putting onto them the responsibility of manipulating the words and expressions known in order to produce statements, questions and answers which express adequately and correctly what they want to say in the circumstances, that the Silent Way is radically different from the outset and is really concerned with what it is to learn another language. I have noticed in students of foreign language a reluctance to use pronouns although pronouns are both vital to normal speaking and extremely economical from the point of view of the learner. "J'en ai deux" is true of "mains, oreilles, yeux, parents, pieds, jambes" and hundreds of other possibilities as well. These possibilities can be pointed out the moment the use of "en" has been mastered with the rods, and allows the student to know what the teacher knows: that although the expression has been introduced through the rods, it will be good for an endless number of other situations.

From the very first lesson students in the Silent Way are using direct and indirect object pronouns, jammed together "donnezlesmoi" in the way they are normally used. How easy then become expressions like "jevouslesai-donnés" later on. My own memories of expressions like these is of a mathematical type formula from which I extracted what I needed, then put them together, turning out something that resembled a child's first effort at collage. *Y En* (like a donkey, I was told) did not come my way for years, at which point I had to open my sentences and squeeze them in. This might seem amusing if language teaching had really changed very much. I envy my students, who not only meet "en" within two weeks of beginning, but who take so little to see what is there for anyone to see: when you use "en" you do not say "réglette" and vice-versa; you do not begin a conversation using "en", it only comes in after the object has been mentioned. And all this can take place without any reference, in any language, to the word "pronoun."

A simple exercise to introduce "en" might go as follows: rods are given out to some of the students and the teacher, holding two of them says: "J'ai deux réglettes et vous en avez une"; a motion with the fingers tells the student he is being asked to comment on the situation from his point of view: "J'ai une réglette et vous en avez deux". Many students have already done enough work on their listening to be able to hear where it is that "en" has been inserted and can work out "j'en ai" without ever having heard it said first.

It takes only as much observation and listening to note what is happening with the expressions "J'ai pris la réglette" and "je l'ai prise."

What pronouns offer us is the possibility of referring to an already mentioned object or person in a shorter form. *Les*, *en*, and *y* are the most economical as they can be used to refer to anything at all. In spite of the fact that pronouns are used everyday by students in their own language and by students who would not dream of saying anything like: "the little boy crossed the street, the little boy went to the corner, the little boy met a man ..." there is often a wariness about using pronouns in French, particularly when "il" and "elle" are first met as referring to all objects and not only people. I have seen many classes where the idea of showing the students the alternatives offered by pronouns is done by using the word *or* or *ou*. This has always seemed a violation of the truth and a very confusing thing to do. One never says anything like "J'ai deux frères ou j'en ai deux" in any language I have come across so far. Secondly, knowing about something is no substitute for being able to use it; and thirdly, it destroys any understanding of what the relationship is between those two expressions.

This can all be covered so quickly and simply with the Silent Way. For example: everyone (or just a couple of students) is given a rod; the teacher says "Ma réglette est rouge" and the students take turns in making a similar statement about their own rod. Once this has been done, the other possessive adjectives can be introduced. Then perhaps everyone can take a new rod and the round is begun again, this time by a student, who may say "Ma réglette est bleue" and the teacher comes in with "La mienne est rouge", and passes to the next student.

This exercise, coming usually within the first couple of hours of instruction, often creates a situation which allows an opportunity to show the students the difference between the Silent Way and other approaches and what it is that is being demanded of them. In the above example, after the teacher has brought in "la mienne" it is not unusual for a student to follow with "et ma réglette est jaune". As this form was quite correct until a minute ago, any student who receives a reject call for this statement would have every right to feel confused. On the other hand, if it is greeted with a shrug, a wave of the hand indicating "well, all right, but listen to this person over here" (indicating another student who seems ready to offer "la mienne") the student can realize that while being correct, the statement can be improved upon. It is then for the student to realize that there is now another possibility and it may take only one or two more examples for all the students to be using it. It only remains then to notice that the person who begins the round cannot start with this new form.

Demonstrative adjectives and pronouns can be dealt with in the same way, by introducing situations where the distance between the speaker and the rods can be easily seen to have a bearing on the words used. The relative pronoun *qui* is also introduced early and it gives us the means of joining several separate sentences and thereby allowing a flow of words in several phrases: "La réglette noire est devant la réglette jaune, qui est devant la réglette ..., qui est devant ...". Once "je l'ai prise" has been learned, "la réglette que j'ai prise" can follow.

There are numerous exercises which can help turn students' awareness to what pronouns do. Gap games (sentences with blanks to be filled in) can be done from mimeoed sheets or the blackboard; they can offer sentences where there are several possible words to be inserted and some where only a particular one will do. Lists of the possibilities can be made by the students individually or by the class as a whole. These can be added to as new words appear. Later, grammatical labels can be attached to these lists and gradually the students can write their own grammar books.

Students can be asked to make their own list of words that replace people and things. When teaching English speakers French it is easy enough to explain directions for an exercise using words which correspond closely to the English words for substitute, replace, personal, list, category, description, etc. A few examples done by the whole class should be enough to get the exercise started.

Jane Orton

2.

I began my work with classes of beginners and of more advanced students who had already learned some French through the Silent Way. Their different levels helped me to discover the steps I had to take in order to make them go from a restricted functional language to an expanding vocabulary.

The beginners still help me understand the difficulties which the intermediate students encounter when trying to use words, expressions or structures which do not seem difficult *to me*. The time they take to understand the meanings, to produce or to feel at ease with the sounds allows me to become aware of the complexity or the ambiguities of the language itself. (For example: "*C'est une* réglette brune. *Cette* réglette est brune.*) I have therefore the task of bringing the students' attention to slightly perceptible yet important differences.

The awareness of homonyms having grammatical implications is one of the main difficulties of French. Many students believe that they have to move their mouth dramatically to get the right pronunciation instead of noticing the similarities of sounds yet the differences of meanings. In the case of the above example I used the context when the work was still oral to guide the learner in acquiring criteria to differentiate the following examples:

Qu'est-ce que *c'est?* — *C'est une* réglette brune.

Cette réglette est brune. — *Celle-ci* est jaune.

Another transformation, such as shift to the plural, can make the point clearer.

Ce sont des réglettes brunes. — *C'est une* réglette brune.

Ces réglettes sont brunes. — *Cette* réglette est brune.

In this, as in many other cases, the spelling is helpful. The visual aspect of the Silent Way of teaching should be taken into account whenever it can resolve a deadlock. It shows the students that they are able to shift from using their ears to using their eyes as well in order to sort things out.

One of the difficulties I met with the more advanced students was the lack of a program in the Silent Way such as textbooks or former exam papers to which I could refer in order to know more accurately the level of proficiency of my students. I found that even the charts did not fully suffice in determining the level of the students. The charts allow the teacher great flexibility in working on different aspects of the language but it is often difficult to know *exactly* what material the class has mastered after encountering it.

I made the mistake of assuming that students had mastered the main French structures because I knew that they had spent several months on them. I had not expected silence after my initial "easy" questions! I was struck by the fact that several students repeatedly stated they did not remember anything from the lessons they had had before the summer vacations.

I soon discovered that I had to correct my assumption that the time spent in the classroom is synonymous with learning. The school year is not a measure of learning. The mood of the class, the attention it gives to the teaching, and the teacher's ability itself are vital in the learning process.

I learned not to assume that my students "should know" even though they had been exposed to the Silent Way for some time. I felt freer to return to earlier lessons so as to remind the students of some basic structures. I helped them *recognize* what they once had known, and how to bring out of their memory linguistic knowledge which was dormant but not forgotten. The task was to make them aware that there is an obvious gap between "being aware" and "mastering." This gap should not be filled by rote exercises or drills, using examples in which one grammatical structure is utilized differently in various cases. Once the students understand the meaning of "Où est la plus petite de ces réglettes?" (and are able to ask and answer this question), they should be urged to ask many questions starting with: "Où est . . . ." and to build up more elaborate sentences with their expanding vocabulary. I found that the students enjoyed hiding objects to make

106

the exercise more real. This provided a good opportunity to learn the past tense.

— *Où est* la montre qui était sur la table?

— J'avais une réglette dans la main. Elle n'y est plus. *Où est-elle* maintenant?

— Les livres *étaient* sous l'armoire. Quelqu'un les *a pris.* Où sont-ils?"

My approach in generating a program was to become sensitive, *here and now* to the needs of these children.

Another difficulty I had to face was with those students who thought that "they ought to know." My job here was to determine the factors which were preventing them from learning. Talking incidentally with a student I noticed that he felt deeply ashamed of his accent in his mother tongue. He then assumed that he could not speak French with "its" proper accent either. His fears, his preconceptions had confused him about two different components of what we call accent, that is to say, the native accent we acquire from our environment and the accent we use in speaking a foreign language, while retaining the conventions of our native tongue. I showed him a few words on the charts going from "*u*ne," to "*vu, pu, pu*is, dep*u*is, *pu*isque, *ju*sque, pl*u*sieurs," and he worked on the "u" sound until he got the correct pronunciation. The following days he spent much time trying to produce the French "r" and all nasalizations such as "an, in on, un." He was able to understand statements in French much better and knew that he was speaking an acceptable French. The work he did then taught me a lot. It showed me how one can correct the mistakes one has been making for a long time (resulting from preconceptions, fear or lack of confidence) as soon as one is conscious of what one is doing.

I was alerted to the fact that some of my students' learning problems were, in fact, errors of my teaching and of judgments on my part. For some time I could not understand why some students who were given visual dictation needed to repeat a broken sentence very quickly instead of putting the words together at a smooth pace. I began to watch my pointer as I grouped words together and noticed that I waved it too quickly, unaware of this confusing gesture.

If a student says: "Combien/de/grandes/réglettes/avez-vous/dans/la main?" I show him how words are linked together. I lift my thumb and the three following fingers, then make him match each one of the four words he said with one finger (Combien/de/grandes/réglettes). Then I bring my fingers together and the student understands that he must do the same with his words. Therefore he can say: "Combien de grandes réglettes" without breaking the flow. Once we have worked similarly with the five other words of this sentence I would bring together the two hands so that the student perceives where are the short stops in it ("Combien de grandes réglettes/avez-vous/dans la main?").

I started to learn that with the Silent Way approach both students and the teacher have to deal with a very subtle mental dynamics, not easily detectable. I found myself increasingly ready to accept being in the background and not the main figure in the show. I know that, the more silent, the more discrete, the more neutral I become, the closer to themselves my students are. The hardest job in the Silent Way is the self control and the alertness it requires all the time. It is a constant challenge. It is this acceptance of the reality of any learning as a reality of life which makes the Silent Way most valuable to my teaching.

Ghislaine Graf

Three years ago, about this time, I realized once again that something wasn't clicking in the ways foreign languages were being taught. I had one particular class — ninth grade, third year French — which was an average class composed of neither brilliant nor particularly ungifted students. We had very close rapport, the class ran smoothly most of the time and the atmosphere was pleasant.

"Why weren't the results better?", I asked myself. We had started together in the seventh grade, and although a number of students were now speaking French quite well and their general knowledge of French was quite good, there were a number of students in this particular class who seemed to have achieved very little for all the effort and time expended. By comparison, I found that the class I had had the previous year, which had also been with me for three years, had a much better knowledge of French. This class had been made up largely of very bright students and I realized that these students were so motivated that they needed the teacher only as a source of information. Any teaching method or approach would have brought good results with this group.

But what about less gifted and less motivated students? I felt that there must be another way to reach the learners, to mobilize their natural ability and curiosity which, in turn, would help them achieve what they set out to do — that is, to learn French. The question was, how to do it?

I was in a somewhat discouraged frame of mind when I was introduced for the first time to the Silent Way. I have since adopted this approach of teaching foreign languages and, although a number of questions remain unresolved, I have the feeling that at least I am on the right road of teaching and that I am getting closer to the goal.

What has happened? The first thing that comes to mind

is that in the classes taught by the Silent Way there is a closer relationship between the learner and the teacher. At the same time, the learner is engaged in the learning process with much greater independence than is the case in the traditional classes. The teacher becomes much more aware of the individual student and his needs through the student's involvement with the material presented, his class participation or lack of it. The whole class becomes quite active and vocal; there is a certain electricity that permeates the classroom. Due to the fact that no books are used while the basics of the language are being studied, the learner cannot get lost in following a text while at the same time his mind might wander off in another direction. The teacher can follow the learner's responses through what he is saying and very often through his facial expressions. New situations which are introduced with the help of the rods trigger spontaneous and simultaneous responses from the class. These responses are an indication to the teacher of how the students relate to what is going on. When one of the learners then comes forward to re-enact the situation in his own way and when he expresses it in his own words, the class as a whole works with him and either accepts or rejects his flow of words. Another learner is always anxious to try to do the scene differently or to add something to what has been said by his fellow learner. I have found that, with a few exceptions, the whole class participates, is *with it*, and very little of the classroom time is wasted.

One might think that because this approach is very demanding of the student, the so-called poorer or average student would be left behind and would give up. This, however, is not the case. The natural curiosity of all learners, I find, makes them want to go on and find the key to learning themselves.

Because of the involvement of the students and because of the unambiguous ways in which new structures are

110

introduced, the students are able to acquire with ease what is traditionally considered difficult.

I would like to cite an example: The teaching of reflexive verbs usually presents quite a problem as there are so many more such verbs in French than in English. In one of my 7th grade classes (beginning French) this hurdle solved itself quite simply: While sitting down I said "je m'assieds sur la chaise." Then I took a hand-mirror and said: "je me regarde," and one little girl immediately said, "vous mettez votre corps sur la chaise," referring back to my first statement. Then when I held the mirror (luckily it had two faces) to a student and to myself I got the utterance "nous nous regardons" from the student and "vous vous regardez" and finally "ils se regardent," respectively, from the class.

We then went through several other reflexive verbs (se lever, se laver, se coucher, etc.) and by the responses of the class and their various statements it was quite obvious that the concept was clear to them. Then I proceeded to put a doll on the chair and one of the students said "Vous l'asseyez sur la chaise."

While the difference in meaning and usage of "se" and "le," "la" and "les" was solved in an apparently simple and uncomplicated manner, it must be born in mind that this was due to the fact that these students had been learning French by the Silent Way for a certain period of time.

Their awareness of the difference between "se" and "le" came as a direct result of their perception of the unambiguous linguistic situations and the sounds which were associated with them.

The most important aspect in using this approach is the respect the teacher must grant the learner and the confidence that the learner develops. As long as the teacher is able to present the material in a manner that is clear and logical from the point of view of the learner,

111

enabling the learner to get excited and involved in the subject matter, the results should be quite different from the ones usually achieved in using other teaching approaches.

Lolita Goldstein

GERMAN

This semester I taught for the first time the Silent Way and therefore am a newcomer to this approach of teaching languages. My few remarks will not deal with specific language problems we encountered but with some changes that occurred within the students and me in the course of these few months. I do not consider our experiences as very original and deep, but they are important to me.

My first surprise in meeting my twenty-two students who had registered for a college beginners' course in German was that they expected the traditional course with grammar explanations, reading and conversation, because they had not been told that this was going to involve different attitudes in learning and teaching. Their eager acceptance spoke well for their flexibility and willingness to do something new. I spoke to them frankly, explaining that they could trust my German since I was a native speaker but that I had taught the traditional language courses for many years and therefore was inexperienced in this new approach. I told them that we would have to face difficult situations together.

I never repented having made these remarks because my doubts concerning myself and not the Silent Way were more than justified. I realized that I could not change over night and that giving up my comfortable power and authority made me feel unsure of myself. This became

113

even apparent physically since the rods seemed to shake with me, falling on the floor, refusing to stand upright guided by my shaking hands. These difficulties, however, subsided after a few days as I started feeling more at ease in my new position. I began to accept my own mistakes just as I became more understanding of my students' mistakes. I often created situations with the rods that were not clear enough, and therefore I saw frustrated faces in front of me. "Ich lege das Stäbchen auf den Tisch, ich habe das Stäbchen auf den Tisch gelegt," went fine, but "Ich werde das Stäbchen auf den Tisch legen," seemed a puzzle until I went to the door, applying the entire situation to the door. "Ich werde die Tür aufmachen," became quite clear as I stood there prepared to open it, yet not opening it. The complicated "Das Stäbchen liegt auf dem Tisch, und ich habe es auf den Tisch gelegt," however, which I had greatly feared, seemed to create few difficulties since the perception was extremely helpful to the students and made any dull memorization quite unnecessary.

The difference between *ein* and *das* was surprisingly painless. I left one single red rod among many white, blue, brown and orange rods. I said: "Nehmen Sie ein blaues Stäbchen, ein weisses Stäbchen" but "*das* rote Stäbchen." Seeing the lonely red rod, most students understood the difference, and those that had understood it, created a similar situation using another color to teach their companions.

My repeated mistake was to persist too frequently in trying to solve the problems right now when I had not been able to make the situation clear instead of postponing the solution and giving myself time to think. To my surprise, however, one of the other students who had seen clearly through my fumbling efforts, would step in and give a helping hand. I heard sighs of relief and smiles brightened the gloomy faces.

114

As the weeks advanced I became aware how little visually oriented I had been all these years. Students made signs that my pocketbook obstructed their view, that the shades had to be pulled down because of the glaring sun making the reading of the charts impossible. They also wanted to recognize the colors of the rods as clearly as possible.

Of course, not every student felt happy right from the start, without the accustomed grammar explanations, and one student left in protest telling me that the Silent Way was not his cup of tea. The great majority stayed, more than in a traditionally taught course. Some of them became much freer, jumping up, seizing the rods to find clarification by setting up a new situation or replacing the rods by other objects. I heard them say: "Mit dem Bleistift, aber mit der Feder," shaking their head at the strange German language. One girl got up waddling like a duck to explain the word "Ente" I had been unable to explain. Yet, I continued to realize that I did not fully listen to the students nor was I often aware of their reactions.

The striking example was a young, strong student who stood beside my desk describing the rods. I heard him ask whether he should continue and not looking at him, I urged him to do so. After a few more words his voice became faint and his face white. He went back to his seat and soon recovered. I asked advice from the students. "Never have a student do this over too long a period, at least not at the beginning," they said I realized that my ears and eyes should have given me warning signals. I was still too bent on good results in the language and not really understanding the person. Such experiences taught me that we were all learning together, each at his or her own pace.

The students were also very willing to help each other, and the competitive spirit so prevalent in many college classes seemed to diminish. I do not mean, of course, that it disappeared. When a student, for example, misspelled the new word "Geld" on the blackboard writing a *t*, they would immediately point to the *und* on the chart. A mispronounced *z* in "zahlen" would provoke shouts of "zwei," "schwarz," reminding him of what he actually already knew. Emotions were often quite strong, frustration as well as delight and excitement when students discovered things by themselves. Once, when in complete despair, I was tempted to give an explanation, they did not want it. They preferred to struggle to find the solution.

During the semester I made an observation that took me by surprise. I had worried so much about this new approach, about my inadequacies and yet this was the class to which I looked forward most when I got up in the morning. What was the reason for it? There are surely many, and I do not understand them all. What I liked was the unexpected event, the unforseen delights and disappointments, the students' active participation, the variety of living experiences. There was an atmosphere of congeniality, of common interest that linked us all together. But I knew that I needed much deeper changes, greater inner freedom to enable students to use their creativity to a much greater extent. As I left my last class of last semester, I felt how much we all had to learn but that we had learned something.

Hilde Jaeckel

model for my own classes, but I soon discovered that I was betraying the whole idea of the Silent Way because I was not taking into consideration the reality of Italian in relation to my class. This is one of the reasons why I don't think it would be possible to work out a teachers' guide: the beginner teacher, overwhelmed by the novelty of the approach would tend to rely heavily on the guide and therefore on the techniques rather than developing his or her own way to use the materials offered.

Instead, one should become aware that there is no magic in the materials per se and that, if necessary, they could all be thrown out and replaced. Nothing is sacred in the Silent Way not even the silence, and to follow the "letter" of the approach (using the rods, the charts, being silent etc., etc.) is no guarantee of really using the Silent Way. It is the "spirit" of the Silent Way that needs to be grasped and followed — as Dr. Gattegno once pointed out — if one wants real learning to take place.

I personally find that the acquisition of the discipline required for becoming independent and truly responsive to the situations and problems arising in my classes is the hardest part of this way of teaching. However, it is also the most rewarding in that the teacher learns and grows in awareness *with* the students. Inevitably, the whole attitude of both students and the teacher changes, and not only toward the subject matter but towards each other. A new atmosphere of trust and tolerance is created where learning becomes the most important part of the class regardless of the roles. Indeed, I have let my students take over and set situations which would trigger the very words I had found impossible to convey. One day while I was trying unsuccessfully to convey the meaning of "ognuno," a student offered the following solution: he took twelve rods and built a tower with them, then said: "Ho costruito una torre con dodici regoli rossi, *ognuno* dei quali è lungo due centimetri." Everybody understood. The word "ognu-

119

no" placed in that particular context could not but convey its meaning with precision and clarity. I had been working with the problem by giving each student a rod and then saying "*ogni* studente ha un regolo," and then "*ognuno* di voi ha un regolo." While the meaning of "ogni" became clear very soon, the meaning of "ognuno" defeated almost everyone. I was all the more surprised when this particular student came out with his solution. It appeared obvious to me that by changing the situation, he proved that he now possessed the word so completely as to be able to manipulate it in the way he wanted.

The Silent Way has taught me how to shift the focus from myself to students. While it relieved me from the anxiety of having to be always under the spotlight, it taught my students two invaluable things:

a. the importance of the personal contribution both in the sense of giving and receiving and in the sense of understanding that finally the responsibility for learning lies only with the learner;

b. the necessity of a strict inner discipline which would allow them to control their functionings in order to be able to communicate with each other.

Thus the girl who kept on saying "arangione" with a nasal "an" was forced to see that unless she made herself *hear* what she was saying, the correct word "arancione" would not come out. The interesting thing was that she was convinced, like the other students, that if someone repeated the word, she would be able to repeat it correctly afterwards. As a matter of fact, the correct repetition of the word served no purpose at all, it was only when she heard herself pronounce the word that progress started, and through a series of self corrections, she soon possessed the word with the pronunciation of a native speaker.

The importance of inner discipline became dramatically clear this year in a class where there were many Spanish speaking students. All of them felt that since they could understand most of what was going on in class, they did not need to pay too much attention. They soon discovered that whenever they tried to say something in Italian, Spanish would come out instead. The discipline to block Spanish proved at times just as hard, if not harder, than the discipline other students without Spanish background needed in order to learn Italian.

The Silent Way is indeed more than a set of tools for teaching a foreign language. It is a way to allow students to observe themselves learn and to discover what their powers of learning are and how they can use them more effectively. It is the succession of these discoveries that makes students exhilarated and desiring to go on, not the particular subject matter. This is why it is important that the teacher give no answers. The results become much less important than the process of learning and the students feel that if they pay attention to the process, they free themselves from fears and inhibitions and the result is inevitably creativity. In talking to students one will get reactions of this kind: "I never thought that mistakes could be very important for learning," or "I really feel that more than learning Italian I am learning how a language is learned," or "this is not really a method it is an attitude towards life."

I, like my students, have always been too concerned with the product, often forgetting the process. Now, I have found that even mastering the skills of a foreign language can be a joy and not just a drudgery and the price to pay for *later* enjoyment of reading the literature and knowing the people of that language. And while it is difficult to free oneself from the bonds of distant rewards and social values, it is encouraging to see that the freer the teacher becomes, the more students respond positively; and eventually even more of the curriculum will be studied, absorbed and assimilated as part of the self.

Cecilia Bartoli Perrault

121

RUSSIAN

Relativity with Respect to Time:
Some Exercises in Awareness
of the Russian Language

In order for language to be used to make adequate
statements about reality, it must have the capacity to
reflect certain universal components which are a part of
that reality. And it is clear from experience that the
universe which surrounds us is subject to the laws of time,
space, and causation. Therefore, it is reasonable to expect
that language, when used to make such statements, will
have the means to take these laws into account. In the
process of working on the techniques of teaching Russian
the Silent Way, I have had the opportunity of exploring
possible uses of rods for developing an awareness of the
first of these laws — time — as it is reflected in the Russian
language. The following is meant to be a short description
and exploration of some of the exercises worked out thus
far.

One great virtue of the colored rods is the unmistakabil-
ity of their physical characteristics and their attraction for
the eye as it concentrates on the manner in which they are
manipulated. For our purposes it is possible to select two
of the rods, let us say a pink one and a yellow one, and to
set up three different situations which will demonstrate in
a concrete and unambiguous way the relativity with
respect to time about which we are concerned.

First, one might take the pink rod and stand it on an otherwise bare table in front of us. After a short pause, one might take the yellow rod and lay it on the table a short distance away from the pink one. After another short pause, one might say in Russian: "*Ja postavil rozovuju prizmu na stol. Potom ja položil žëltuju prizmu na stol.*"

Second, one might take the pink rod in the right hand and the yellow rod in the left hand, and hold them above the table. Then one might begin lowering the pink one, and before it reaches the table, lower the yellow one all the way to the table ... after which the pink one, too, would reach the table. After a short pause, one might say in Russian: "*Kogda ja opuskal rozovuju prizmu na stol, ja opustil žëltuju prizmu na stol.*"

Third, one might take the pink rod in the right hand and the yellow rod in the left hand. Then one might slowly stand the pink rod and slowly lay the yellow rod on the table simultaneously. After a short pause, one might say in Russian: "*Kogda ja stavil rozovuju prizmu na stol, ja klal žëltuju prizmu na stol.*"

Thus it can be seen that, in response to three different combinations of movements with the hands and rods, three different statements in the Russian language were generated which offered possible ways of taking into account what happened. By coordinating what was seen, heard, and done, even a person with little or no knowledge of Russian could explore the content of the above statements.* Intuitively, the notions of sequentiality and simultaneity, as well as the notion of completion of one action within another, are evoked because of what is taken in by the eye. How these notions are dealt with by the Russian language can then be investigated by referring to the utterances taken in by the ear. It is then possible for

---

*Written here in a standard, Latin-character transliteration in order to provide a point of entry for someone interested in such exploration, but who would find the traditional Cyrillic characters too confusing.

understanding to take place once the mind has coordinated what was seen and what was heard.

These three exercises might soon lead to others, in which other components of the situation were altered, which in turn would necessitate altering the statements made in Russian. Here it is enough to investigate what changes might have been brought about if, for the three examples of manipulations given above, the statement in Russian had come before the action: *"Ja postavlju rozovuju prizmu na stol. Potom ja položu žëltuju prizmu na stol." "Kogda ja budu opuskat' rozovuju prizmu na stol, ja opušču žëltuju prizmu na stol." "Kogda ja budu stavit' rozovuju prizmu na stol, ja budu klast' žëltuju prizmu na stol."*

Or if it had come during the action: *"Ja stavlju rozovuju prizmu na stol. Potom ja kladu žëltuju prizmu na stol." "Kogda ja opuskaju rozovuju prizmu na stol, ja opuskaju žëltuju prizmu na stol." "Kogda ja stavlju rozovuju prizmu na stol, ja kladu žëltuju prizmu na stol."*

It can be seen that the variety of situations possible with the colored rods is limited here only by the imagination of the teacher and the willingness of the learner to take up new challenges. Out of such exercises will grow an awareness, and ultimately a mastery of the way in which the Russian language takes into account relativity with respect to time in the universe of people, things, and action.

«Я поставил розовую призму на стол. Потом я положил жёлтую призму на стол.»

«Когда я опускал розовую призму на стол, я опустил жёлтую призму на стол.»

«Когда я ставил розовую призму на стол, я клал жёлтую призму на стол.»

«Я поставлю розовую призму на стол. Потом я положу жёлтую призму на стол.»

«Когда я буду опускать розовую призму на стол, я опущу жёлтую призму на стол.»

Когда я буду ставить розовую призму на стол, я буду класть жёлтую призму на стол.»

«Я ставлю розовую призму на стол. Потом я кладу жёлтую призму на стол.»

«Когда я опускаю розовую призму на стол, я опускаю жёлтую призму на стол.»

«Когда я ставлю розовую призму на стол, я кладу жёлтую призму на стол.»

James Karambelas

SPANISH

1

A Silent Lesson

I do not think I fully understood the importance of a silent teacher until I worked in tandem with Dr. Gattegno, teaching Spanish. I did this on three occasions, twice during three day intensive seminars, of about 21 hours each, and the third time during a five week training seminar for the teachers of an experimental public school in New York City's Bronx.

Dr. Gattegno conducted the seminars and I would only provide the words necessary to describe different situations that he would create with the rods. Being "the voice," and not the teacher, I found myself in a special situation of someone who is partially involved in the learning process of a group of people while the actual teaching was done by someone else. I could, therefore, observe the resulting phenomenon, though always on my toes to come in when asked to do so. It was then that I realized what tremendous amount of language learning can take place when the students are asked and, what is more important, allowed to use the richness of their own knowledge of language learning which they had acquired while learning their native tongue.

One of the lessons will especially remain with me because it was a crucial moment in my own growing — a growing that any Silent Way teacher knows is a lifelong experience. It was during the sixth lesson of Spanish for the Bronx teachers, an equivalent of about six hours in the language, that I became aware of the fact that for a period of one and a half hours I was asked to say only two words: *dentro* and *fuera*.

During all this time the students were constantly using Spanish while responding to Dr. Gattegno's silent directions in gestures. But at times they also took the initiative of changing the situations presented to them, since the teacher, though constantly in control of the lesson, gave the students the freedom to match their own perceptions with whatever knowledge of the new language they had acquired. They discovered that they knew far more than they had thought, since the freedom to experiment revealed their awareness of the correct Spanish constructions.

How was it possible that I was only asked to utter two words during that particular lesson and what were the students able to do with these words?

Since the use of the colored rods allows introduction of unambiguous situations through which the students can perceive various kinds of special relationships, at this point they were able to make the following statements:

a. Tome una regleta azul, dos amarillas y todas las rojas, deme a mí las amarillas, dele a él las rojas y a ella la azul.

b. Una regleta negra está tumbada encima de una regleta azul que está de pie encima de una anaranjada que está tumbada encima de la mesa.

c. El color de mi regleta es amarillo. ¿De qué color es su regleta?

d. ¿De qué color son las regletas que están encima de la mesa?

e. Esta regleta negra está aquí, esa azul está ahí, aquella roja está allí.

f. La regleta azul está a la derecha de la negra y a la izquierda de la roja.

These are only a few examples of the many situations they were able to describe with the elements they were given. The descriptions always corresponded to the students' own perception of the situation and were not repetition of the teacher's statement.

As an illustration of this let us consider examples e. and f. In e. the two students who sat at the opposite sides of the table, facing each other, would be asked to describe what apparently was the same situation.*

But, while example e. would be accepted from student A, student B would describe the situation as:

Esta regleta roja está aquí, esa azul está ahí, aquella negra está allí.

A and B were only able to say the same thing for the blue rod, while for the red and the black ones their perceptions of the situation were different.

If we can now consider students C and D, facing each other, sitting at the two other opposite sides of the table, we will realize that their description of the situation created with the rods would have to be different from those given by A and B. In our lesson, C was able to say:

1. La regleta azul está entre las regletas roja y negra;

2. La regleta azul está a la derecha de la roja y a la izquierda de la negra;

*There were obviously three rods on the table between students A (on the left) and B (on the right), the black rod being closest to A, the red closest to B, and the blue in the middle.

128

3. La regleta negra está a la derecha de la azul que está a la derecha de la roja;

4. La regleta roja está a la izquierda de la azul que está a la izquierda de la negra.

When it was D's turn to describe what was in front of him he would reverse the order of the adjectives given by C.

Thus the students had developed criteria which allowed them to use the elements of the language they were provided with in order to express their perception in accurate Spanish.

By the same token students A and B were also able to say the following. A:

1. La regleta roja está delante de la azul que está delante de la negra;

2. La regleta negra está detrás de la azul que está detrás de la roja,

while B would use the adjectives and prepositions which were appropriate to his perception.

Therefore, since they had already worked with: "encima de" and "debajo de", "delante de", "detrás de", etc., at the time of the sixth lesson, they already had enough of a feeling for the language to know that "dentro", when used in a situation similar to the one which was presented to them, would not function in isolation but would be followed by the preposition "de."

The situation they were asked to describe showed a black rod standing in the box. They knew the word for "box" (*caja*) which they had used before, but they didn't know how to say "inside" so, once they had said:

La regleta negra está de pié . . .

the teacher turned to me and I uttered:

129

... dentro ...

which allowed them to go on with:

dentro de la caja.

When the rod was placed outside the box the students themselves took the initiative of describing the situation, stopping only at the point when they needed the word *fuera*. Once this word was provided it was integrated and they continued with their description.

I have taught languages and worked with teachers long enough to know that the immediate response to this experience from many of the readers will be: "This is all right for these very simple situations and at a beginner's stage. But what about the introduction of verbs?"

If this is in fact a question for the reader, I would first ask him to reconsider it, since the situations described above imply mastery in the use of adverbs, prepositions and adverbial phrases which are usually difficult to present within a realistic situation. After years of traditional study of English it was still a puzzle for me that I had to say: "I arrived in New York" and not "to New York". The logic of my own language told me that to arrive is a verb expressing motion, therefore it should be followed by a preposition that implies direction such as *to*, and not the one implying place or location such as *in*. I was always asked "to remember" what I had to say and never to block my own language while studying another one.

Still, the question of how would you go about introducing verbs with the rods is a very relevant one and I would like to make a contribution towards its answer, though it will always be a question for us to work on and one that every teacher will have to answer for himself.

I can not give advice in this area, but I can share with other teachers what I do in order to tackle such a difficult problem as the introduction of the subjunctive in Spanish, which seems to be a threatening ghost for many teachers of Spanish. A ghost threatening enough to have pushed some teachers to make their students believe that they can speak Spanish without knowing the subjunctive.

Let us examine the following exercise.

If the teacher asks some of his students to sit in a circle and gives each of them a different rod he may turn to one of them and tell him:

Cuando yo le dé una regleta azul Ud me dará una marrón,

putting special emphasis on "*cuando* yo le *dé*" and "me *dará.*" Then he will give the student the blue rod with one hand and keep the other hand open in an expecting manner. It may certainly be argued that the students will understand this as a future tense and this is perfectly acceptable since the sequence introduced is in fact present subjunctive — simple future indicative. My experience is that once the students begin to listen analytically to the consistent presence of "cuando" in every case, and to recognize the fact that this new "dé" is quite different from the "doy" of the present indicative, which they have heard before, they begin to realize that there is something about this sequence that is different from the present-future sequence of the indicative. After a while they see that the second action is conditional to the first one but that there is also a quality of simultaneity in the sequence.

Further experience may be provided with situations such as:

1. Cuando yo tome dos regletas verdes Ud tomará tres rojas.
2. Cuando el ponga sus regletas encima de la mesa yo le daré las mías, etc.

Once enough experience has been provided with this sequence, the teacher can introduce preterit perfect subjunctive followed by simple conditional (potencial simple in Spanish).

For example:

¿Si yo le diera una regleta anaranjada,
Ud me daría dos amarillas?

When this has been presented through a situation created with the rods (because of their special quality, which I call austere as well as mesmerizing) the transfer to other verbs and other situations is a very simple matter. Indeed there is no difference in spirit between the example given above and the following one:

Si Ud fuera a Europa ¿visitaría Córcega?

or in the case of the first example:

Cuando yo vaya a Europa, visitaré Córcega.

I have worked with students of different age groups and different linguistic backgrounds, and I know that when the spirit of the Silent Way is respected, and the techniques and materials used properly these and other problems are resolved easily. This is possible because the reality of the learning process is the guide for the teacher.

Maria del Carmen Gagliardo

2.

The use of the colored rods in the Silent Way makes it possible to introduce at the same time, in Spanish, the use — as auxiliary verbs — of the present indicative of the verb *ir* with the infinitive of a verb like *poner*; of the present indicative of the verb *estar* with the present participle of *poner* and of the present indicative of the verb *haber* with the past participle of *poner.*

Most of my experience has been in giving intensive 21 hour Spanish seminars on the weekend, with five hours on Friday evening, eight hours on Saturday and eight hours on Sunday. The cumulative offect of the intensive seminars makes the students progress more quickly than they would if they were receiving one hour of class time daily, for 21 days. For example, in a class where I taught only three hours once a week, I introduced the above pattern on the 20th hour. In a seminar, however, I usually introduce the same pattern around the 15th hour. I undertake this sort of exercise only after I am quite sure that the students have had other experiences with the verbs *ir*, *poner*, *estar* and *haber* and after they have had numerous opportunities to listen to, as well as to generate long sentences in Spanish, so that the sounds of Spanish are familiar to them. By this time, the students have actually had the experience of reading, writing and developing criteria for spelling in Spanish.

One can begin by taking the bag that the rods come in and identifying it for the students. Then one can open the bag wide, empty it on the table, and without touching the rods, say

Voy a poner las regletas negras dentro de la bolsa, una a una.

Immediately after saying this (without expecting the students to respond), put the rods in the bag, one by one, saying:

Las estoy poniendo, una a una,

continuing to say this until all the rods are in the bag. Then one can say:

Las he puesto.

133

Then inviting a student to perform the same action (using different colored rods) the teacher says to the class

Va a poner las regletas amarillas dentro de la bolsa, una a una.

If the previous steps have been made clearly, and the student has the proper criteria, he or she will say:

Voy a poner las regletas amarillas dentro de la bolsa, una a una.

The student will begin putting the rods into the bag, one by one, saying:

Las estoy poniendo, una a una.

Some students may say to their neighbor or to the teacher:

Las está poniendo, una a una.

After all the rods have been put in the bag, the teacher can make a gesture of finality with respect to the action. The student says:

Las he puesto.

His or her classmates say with the teacher if they are not yet secure in what they are saying:

Las ha puesto.

This sort of exercise can be repeated by another student or by the teacher by simply changing the color and the number of the rods. The number of people performing the action can be changed as well, allowing for work in the conjugations of the auxiliary verb *haber*, and for the students themselves to generate the second person and third person plurals. After some proficiency is achieved, the exercise of reading on the charts and writing what has been done in a situation can be enlightening in terms of spelling and the logical manner in which *haber* is conjugated.

Verbs for this particular exercise should be the kind whose action is easily perceived; action that can be separated clearly between the expression of the intent to act, the actual action and the expression of what has been done. (I have successfully used verbs such as *tomar*, *escribir*, *construir* and *revolver* with this exercise.) *Encender* is an example of a verb *not* to be used in the beginning because the time between the actual action and the expression of what has been done is so short that the voice cannot make a statement about what is being done before the action is completed.

The rationale for using an irregular verb like *poner* instead of a regular verb in the beginning is that in Spanish, many of the most frequently used verbs are irregular. Therefore, the students may more readily accept the existence of irregularities in the present and past participles if the first ones they meet are irregular.

Exercises that I have used after the one with *poner* to give the students further experience with *ar*, *er* and *ir* verbs are ones that begin with:

Le voy a dar las regletas amarillas, una a una.

   and

Voy a construir un muro con las regletas rojas.

After the students have discovered how some *ar*, *er*, and *ir* verbs form the present and past participles they can become aware of the fact that they know how to form the participles for any verb. This can be done by asking them to make a table of participles.

The students can be asked to think of the verbs they have worked with in the preceding exercises and to put them on the chalkboard. They can be directed to group the verbs according to similar endings, (*ar* ending verbs

135

together in a column, for example). The list they produce may look somewhat as follows:

tomar	poner	escribir
caminar	leer	abrir
cerrar		

Then the following can be put on the board:

1. voy a ——ar   voy a ——er   voy a ——ir
2. estoy ——ando   estoy ——iendo   estoy ——iendo
3. he ——ado   he ——ido   he ——ido

(one way of working is to fill in the first blank between *voy* and *ar* and ask the students to fill in the other blanks).

After this, one can then give the students *ar*, *er* and *ir* verbs they have not heard before, so they can practice using the table. In the *er* and *ir* column certain irregularities in the participles can be either given by the teacher or by students who already know what they are. The list may look as follows:

poner — puesto	escribir — escrito
leer — leyendo	abrir — abierto
volver — vuelto	morir — muerto
hacer — hecho	cubrir — cubierto
romper — roto	decir — dicho

The above table has value in that it serves to consolidate what the students have already gotten from the use of the rods in the exercises. Students with whom I have worked using the preceding exercises and table showed a matter-of-fact confidence about the forming of the present and past participles. I have found this to be true even when students have been engaged in free conversation. This ability results from the silence on the part of the teacher, the use of the rods which brings clarity, and because teachers respect their students' intelligence and their right to discovery. I have seen that it is possible for students to gain a lot from a little with the Silent Way, and in a much shorter time than seems required by other ways of working.

Rosalyn Bennett

3.

Teaching Some Aspects of the Subjunctive Mood in Elementary Spanish

The use of the colored rods during the first phase of a Silent Way course permits the teacher to create carefully controlled, unambiguous situations which, on the one hand, illustrate the meanings of those words which constitute the basic functional vocabulary of the language, and, on the other, challenge the students to use those words much as a native speaker would. In the case of Spanish this includes the relatively complex verb forms and subtleties of meaning of the subjunctive mood. The following examples illustrate how the rods might be used to teach some aspects of the subjunctive mood in Spanish I classes.

As early as the second class meeting the students are introduced to imperatives such as "Tome (or "Toma", depending upon the age of the students) una regleta roja" and "Tome una regleta rosada y póngala aquí." After several additional classes students are quite comfortable giving and performing such relatively complex requests as "Tome dos regletas negras y una verde-claro; a mí deme

137

una negra; a ella dele la verde claro; ponga la otra aquí, por favor." In subsequent classes, after the students have learned other commands as well as some words describing spatial relationships and some tenses of the indicative mood, it is quite possible for the teacher to recreate a situation in which a student is challenged to ask the teacher to do something. For example, the student, Roberto, asks the teacher, "Tome una regleta roja." Before taking a red rod, however, the teacher looks at the rest of the class and begins the observation, "Roberto quiere que ..." and guide's Roberto's classmates in constructing the subordinate clause ". . . Ud. tome una regleta roja." At this point the teacher could have Roberto make the same observation, first to the teacher (Quiero que Ud. tome una regleta roja"), then to his classmates ("Quiero que Señor ———— tome una regleta roja"), and then have the students make the observation to Roberto ("Quieres que Señor ———— tome una regleta roja"), to the teacher (Roberto quiere que Ud. tome una regleta roja"), and finally to other students ("Roberto quiere que Señor ———— tome una regleta roja"). Slight variations of this same situation can be made by challenging several students to give and carry out requests to take one or several rods. In this way many sentences can be created which clearly illustrate the formation and use of the verbs "querer" and "tomar" in the present tense of the indicative and subjunctive moods respectively. Additional situations can be created to give the students practice in using other verbs such as "poner", "meter", "levantarse", "sentarse", "ir", "venir", "salir", and "volver", to mention a few, in all of their present subjunctive forms. After additional practice, the teacher can challenge his students further by asking them to describe the volition *after* the action has been performed, thus permitting the use of other tenses of both the indicative and subjunctive moods. A series of observations of the simple act of sitting down, for example, could challenge the students to form some or all of the following sentences: "Ud. quiere que nosotros le digamos a Ud. que se siente", "Siéntese", "Ud. va a sentarse", "Ud. se sentó", "Queríamos que Ud. se sentara."

Additional situations can be devised to show other uses of "querer". The teacher might point out on the charts the sentence, "Quiero tomar dos regletas negras", and then perform the action, thus showing the use of the infinitive after "querer" when there is no change of subject. In other situations, refusal to obey a command can also illustrate the use of the infinitive ("Alberto no quiere tomar una regleta blanca"), as well as the special meaning of "querer" in the preterit ("Ramón y Roberto no quisieron tomar las regletas verde-claro"). The possible variations are limited only by the imaginations of the teacher and the students and the structure of the language.

Situations which illustrate other uses of the subjunctive mood can be created with the rods. The teacher can introduce an element of uncertainty by placing a rod, not visible to the students, beneath a cloth on his desk. The students can be fairly certain by the shape of the lump under the cloth that a rod has been placed there, but, after asking several students to describe what they are looking at, it becomes readily apparent to everyone that the one variable in the observations concerns the color of the rod under the cloth. A situation has thus been created which requires the use of "creer" (or its negative form, or "dudar") to describe the differing opinions of the various students. The teacher can then signal to two students with differing opinions to join him behind his desk. After eliciting their observations (which might be: "Ud. puso una regleta verde-claro debajo del paño," from one student, Pablo; and "Ud. puso una regleta amarilla debajo del paño," from another, Antonio), the teacher can then introduce the clause, "Pablo cree que . . ." and have Pablo's classmates construct the subordinate clause ". . . la

139

regleta es verde-claro," and subsequently, pointing to Pablo and to the words "no" and "amarilla" (Antonio's choice) on the word charts, have Pablo and his classmates construct the sentences, "Yo . . . (or "Pablo") no creo ("cree") que la regleta sea amarilla." Slight changes in this situation can now be made to use other forms of "creer", and to introduce "sino" ("No cree que sea amarilla sino verde-claro."). Here again the possibilities are limited only by the imagination of the teacher and the students and the structure of the language.

As we have seen, the rods can be used to create situations which challenge the student to give and carry out commands and to make observations of a reality which they perceive or believe to be true. In addition reference to the absent rods provides opportunities to create situations which are contrary to fact and conditional in nature. The teacher, holding a single blue rod in his hand, elicits the observation, "Ud. tiene una regleta azul."; then, motioning to two more blue rods on the table in front of him, and holding two fingers up next to the rod in his hand, makes the statement, "Si tuviera dos más tendría tres." In another situation the teacher might place a yellow rod upright on his desk and elicit the observation, "Hay una regleta amarilla en la mesilla; tiene cinco centímetros de alto." The teacher could then make an observation, either orally or by visual dictation on the charts, "Si fuera azul tendría nueve centímetros de alto." Simple variations using different rods will challenge the students to make their own slightly different observations of these situations which will immediately indicate to the teacher which students have built a mental structure of the words needed to describe the situation and which have not. Based on this simple testing device the teacher can then provide additional practice for those students who need it.

Contrary-to-fact and conditional situations can be created in other ways. The days of the week, for example, can be represented by seven rods standing approximately ten centimeters apart, across the middle of the teacher's desk. The teacher shows the students a calendar and establishes the convention that the first rod to the students' left represents "domingo". He then works with them on the names of the days both orally and in writing. In subsequent classes he maintains the "domingo" convention and establishes others: the rod moved toward the students to the very edge of the desk represents "hoy", and, in progression, the next rod, moved only halfway to the edge of the desk to draw attention to it, represents "mañana", and so on. Similarly, the rod on the other side of the one representing "hoy" will represent "ayer"; the next, "anteayer", and so forth. At first, the reality required by the particular day on which the exercise is done, is respected. In this way, students practice their newly acquired vocabulary concerning the names of the days of the week and their relationships to one another, as well as the present, future, and preterit forms of "ser" in the indicative mood. In subsequent classes the teacher can manipulate the rods in such a way as to create situations which contradict the temporal reality which, until then, had been respected, thus paving the way for use of contrary to fact and conditional statements. On a Friday, for example, the teacher might move the fourth rod, "miércoles", to the very edge of the desk ("hoy" according to the convention which had been established in previous classes and respected until then). Initial responses might be, "Hoy es miércoles", or "Anteayer fue miércoles." In dealing with the first sentence, the teacher might simply wait until the student realizes on his own, the falseness of the statement, or he might direct the student's attention to the calendar on the wall to remind him of the temporal reality; with the second, the teacher might wait again, or he might move the rod halfway back toward the middle of the desk, thus making the position of the rod

141

conform with the student's observation. The teacher might then return "miércoles" to its original position in line with the other six and move "jueves" out to the edge of the desk ("hoy"). Aware once again of the conventions of the game, the students might remain silent, unable to describe the unfamiliar situation; more likely than not, however, one or several students will observe simply, "Hoy no es jueves." After moving the rod representing "viernes" out halfway to the edge of the desk ("mañana"), the teacher can then point to "jueves" and give the students the first word of the sentence which describes the contrary-to-fact conditional situation created by the position of the rods: "Si ...". At the appropriate time the teacher provides the other new words needed by the students: "... fuera ... sería ...". After sufficient practice with other days of the week, the teacher can then create situations requiring the use of the past perfect subjunctive and the conditional perfect indicative: "Si ayer hubiera sido sábado, anteayer habría sido viernes"; or "Si anteayer hubiera sido martes, el día anterior habría sido lunes." Thus, the position of the rods transforms abstract ideas into concrete realities and permits students to form mental structures linking the meaning illustrated by the rods directly with the flow of words.

The situations described above are but a few examples of how the rods can be used to illustrate some aspects of the subjunctive mood in Spanish I classes and how the students can be challenged to use Spanish much as a native speaker would; that is to say, with an awareness of the meaning symbolized by the words and an ability to make the necessary changes and permutations as required by their perception of the situation. Because students are challenged to function intellectually as they did while learning their native language, they find this way of working reasonable, creative, effective, and enjoyable. Examples of sentences "created" by ninth grade students of Spanish I in some of these and in other situations are reproduced on the following pages.

In the future other Silent Way teachers of Spanish will devise other, perhaps more imaginative uses of the rods in teaching these and other aspects of the language. Such creative innovation is completely possible in this approach to learning; indeed, it is desirable and should be shared with others.

Robert L. Coe

♥

Español I
Señor Coe

1. Ud. apagó las luces después de entrar en la clase.
2. Antes de apagar las luces, Ud. entró en la clase.
3. Antes de abrir la puerta, Alberto encendió las luces.
4. Después de encender las luces, Alberto abrió la puerta.
5. Yo encendí las luces antes de abrir la puerta.
6. Quiero un trago de agua.
7. Pedro salió de la clase porque quería un trago de agua.
8. Siéntese.
9. Siéntate.
10. Ud. va a sentarse.
11. Ud. quiere que nosotros le digamos a Ud. que se siente.
12. Le dijimos que Ud. se sentara.
13. Quiero que Pable se levante.
14. Después de enseñarnos la regleta amarilla Ud. me dijo a mí que viniera aquí.
15. Levántate.

16. Guillermo me dijo que me levantara.
17. Hay dos regletas marrón en la mesilla porque Ud. las puso allí.
18. Diego le dijo a Eduardo que se levantara porque quería (que se levantara).
19. Te levantaste porque Diego te dijo a tí que te levantaras.

Español I
Señor Coe

1. Había tres regletas rojas debajo del paño.
2. Diego y yo creemos que es azul.
3. Ellos creen que es azul.
4. No hay ninguna regleta debajo del paño.
5. Creo que la regleta es anaranjada.
6. Antonio no cree que sea negra, sino azul.
7. Antonio cree que la regleta es azul.
8. Creo que es azul.
9. (Roberto) duda que sea azul.
10. Creo que son dos amarillas.
11. Dudas que sea negra.
12. Dudo que la regleta sea negra.
13. No tenía razón.
14. ¿Quién creía que la regleta fuera azul?
15. Creo que es amarilla.
16. No creo que la regleta sea verde claro.
17. No creo que la regleta sea verde oscuro.
18. Sé que es verde oscuro porque Ramón levantó el paño y la vi.
19. El sabe que es verde oscuro.